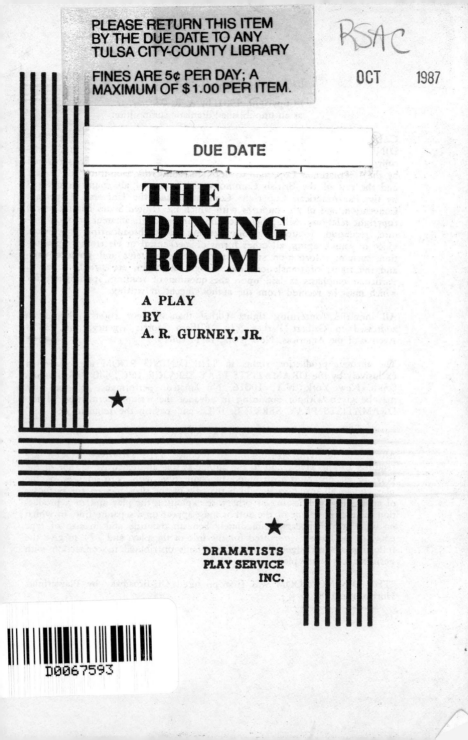

THE DINING ROOM

A PLAY
BY
A. R. GURNEY, JR.

★

★

**DRAMATISTS
PLAY SERVICE
INC.**

SPECIAL NOTE

THE DINING ROOM was first produced at the Studio Theatre of Playwrights Horizons, in New York City, opening January 31, 1981, with the following cast:

1st ACTOR: Remak Ramsay 1st ACTRESS: Lois de Banzie

2nd ACTOR: John Shea   2nd ACTRESS: Ann McDonough

3rd ACTOR: W.H. Macy   3rd ACTRESS: Pippa Pearthree

It was directed by David Trainer. Loren Sherman designed the set, Deborah Shaw the costumes, and Frances Aronson the lighting. The production stage manager was M. A. Howard. Eternal thanks to them all.

3

CASTING SUGGESTIONS:

If a cast of six is used, and there are strong arguments for using this number, the following casting of the roles has proved to be workable and successful:

1st ACTOR: Father, Michael, Brewster, Grandfather, Stuart, Gordon, David, Harvey, and Host

2nd ACTOR: Client, Howard, Pyschiatrist, Ted, Paul, Ben, Chris, Jim, Dick, and Guest

3rd ACTOR: Arthur, Boy, Architect, Billy, Nick, Fred, Tony, Standish, and Guest

1st ACTRESS: Agent, Mother, Carolyn, Sandra, Dora, Margery, Beth, Kate, Claire, Ruth

2nd ACTRESS: Annie, Grace, Peggy, Nancy, Sarah, Harriet, Emily, Annie, and Guest

3rd ACTRESS: Sally, Girl, Ellie, Aggie, Winkie, Old Lady, Helen, Meg, Bertha, and Guest

4

The play takes place in a dining room—or rather, many dining rooms. The same dining room furniture serves for all: a lovely burnished, shining dining room table; two chairs, with arms, at either end; two more, armless, along each side; several additional matching chairs, placed so as to define the walls of the room. Upstage somewhere, a sideboard, with a mirror over it.

Upstage, Left, a swinging door leads to the pantry and kitchen. Upstage, Right, an archway leads to the front hall and the rest of the house. But we should see no details from these other rooms. Both entrances should be masked in such a way as to suggest a limbo outside the dining room.

There should be a good, hardwood floor, possibly parquet, covered with a good, warm oriental rug.

A sense of the void surrounds the room. It might almost seem to be surrounded by a velvet-covered low-slung chain on brass stanchions, as if it were on display in some museum, many years from now.

Since there are no walls to the dining room, windows should be suggested through lighting. The implication should be that there are large French doors Downstage, and maybe windows along another wall.

Since the play takes place during the course of a day, the light should change accordingly.

The play requires a cast of six—three men, three women —and seems to work best with this number. Conceivably

5

it could be done with more, but it would be impossible to do with fewer. The various roles should be assigned democratically; there should be no emphasis on one particular type of role. It might be good to cast the play with people of different ages, sizes, and shapes, as long as they are all good actors.

It would seem to make sense to end the play with the same actors playing Ruth, Annie, and the Host as played Mother, Annie, and Father in the breakfast scene in Act I.

For costumes, it is suggested that the Men wear simple, conservative suits, or jackets and slacks, which can be modified as required. For more informal scenes, for example, an actor might appear in shirt sleeves, or a sweater. Women's costumes might seem to pose a more complicated problem but again the best solution turns out to be the simplest: each actress may wear the same simple, classically styled dress—or skirt and blouse—throughout, with perhaps an occasional apron when she plays a maid. There is hardly enough time between scenes for actors to fuss with changes or accessories, and there is an advantage in being as simple and straightforward as possible.

The place-mats, glassware, china, and silverware used during the course of the play should be bright, clean, and tasteful. We should only see used what is absolutely necessary for a particular scene. Actual food, of course, should not be served. The thing to remember is that this is not a play about dishes, or food, or costume changes, but rather a play about people in a dining room.

The blending and overlapping of scenes have been carefully worked out to give a sense of both contrast and flow. When there is no blending of scenes, one should follow another as quickly as possible. The play should never degenerate into a series of blackouts.

6

THE DINING ROOM

*No one on stage. The dining room furniture sparkles in
the early morning light. Voices from off R. Then a woman
real estate Agent and her male Client appear in the doorway. Both wear raincoats.*

AGENT. . . . and the dining room.

CLIENT. Oh boy.

AGENT. You see how these rooms were designed to catch the
early morning light?

CLIENT. I'll say.

AGENT. French doors, lovely garden, flowering crabs. Do you
like gardening?

CLIENT. Used to.

AGENT. imagine, imagine having a long, leisurely breakfast
in here.

CLIENT. As opposed to instant coffee on Eastern Airlines.

AGENT. Exactly. You know this is a room after my own heart.
I grew up in a dining room like this. Same sort of furniture.
Everything.

CLIENT. So did I.

AGENT. Then here we are. Welcome home. (*Pause.*)

CLIENT. What are they asking again?

AGENT. Make an offer. I think they'll come down. (*Another
pause.*)

CLIENT. Trouble is, we'll never use this room.

AGENT. Oh now.

CLIENT. We won't. The last two houses we lived in, my wife
used the dining room table to sort the laundry.

7

AGENT. Oh dear.

CLIENT. Maybe you'd better show me something more contemporary.

AGENT. That means something farther out. How long have we got to find you a home?

CLIENT. One day.

AGENT. And how long will the corporation keep you here, after you've found it?

CLIENT. Six months to a year.

AGENT. Oh then definitely we should look farther out. (*She opens the kitchen door.*) You can look at the kitchen as we leave.

CLIENT. You shouldn't have shown me this first.

AGENT. I thought it was something to go by.

CLIENT. You've spoiled everything else.

AGENT. Oh no. We'll find you something if we've got all day. But wasn't it a lovely room?

CLIENT. Let's go, or I'll buy it! (*They both exit through the kitchen door as a Brother comes in from the hall, followed by his Sister. Both are middle-aged. His name is Arthur, hers is Sally.*)

ARTHUR. The dining room.

SALLY. Yes...

ARTHUR. Notice how we gravitate right to this room.

SALLY. I know it.

ARTHUR. You sure mother doesn't want this stuff in Florida?

SALLY. She hardly has room for what she's got. She wants us to take turns. Without fighting.

ARTHUR. We'll just have to draw lots then.

SALLY. Unless one of us wants something, and one of us doesn't.

ARTHUR. We have to do it today.

SALLY. Do you think that's enough time to divide up a whole house?

ARTHUR. I have to get back, Sal. (*He looks in the sideboard.*) We'll draw lots and then go through the rooms taking turns. (*He brings out a silver spoon.*) Here. We'll use this salt spoon. (*He shifts it from hand to hand behind his back, then holds out two fists.*) Take your pick. You get the spoon, you get the dining room.

SALLY. You mean you want to start here?

ARTHUR. Got to start somewhere. (*Sally looks at his fists. Annie, a Maid, comes out from the kitchen to set the table for breakfast. She sets placemats at either end and two coffee cups, with saucers. Sally and Arthur take no notice of her. Annie then leaves.*)

SALLY. (*Not choosing.*) You mean you want the dining room?

ARTHUR. Yeah.

SALLY. What happened to the stuff you had?

ARTHUR. Jane took it. It was part of the settlement.

SALLY. If you win, where will you put it.

ARTHUR. That's my problem, Sal.

SALLY. I thought you had a tiny apartment.

ARTHUR. I'll find a place.

SALLY. I mean your children won't want it.

ARTHUR. Probably not.

SALLY. Then where on earth . . . ?

ARTHUR. Come on, Sal. Choose. (*He holds out his fists again. She chooses. Arthur lowers his hands. Annie comes in from the kitchen, bringing the morning paper. She puts it at the head of the table and then leaves.*) You don't want it.

SALLY. Of course I want it!

ARTHUR. I mean you already have a perfectly good dining room.

SALLY. Not as good as this.

ARTHUR. You mean you want two dining rooms?

SALLY. I'd give our old stuff to Debbie.

ARTHUR. To Debbie?

SALLY. She's our oldest child.

ARTHUR. Does Debbie want a dining room?

SALLY. She might.

ARTHUR. In a condominium?

SALLY. She might.

ARTHUR. In Denver?

SALLY. She just might, Arthur. (*A Father comes in from the*

9

right. He settles comfortably at the head of the table, unfolds his newspaper importantly.)
ARTHUR. (*Shuffling the spoon behind his back again. Then holding out his fists.*) I don't want to fight. Which hand? (*Sally starts to choose, then stops.*)
SALLY. Are you planning to put it in storage?
ARTHUR. I might.
SALLY. I checked on that. That costs an arm and a leg.
ARTHUR. So does shipping it to Denver. (*He holds out his fists.*)
FATHER. (*Calling to kitchen.*) Good morning, Annie.
SALLY. (*Almost picking a hand, then stopping.*) I know what will happen if you win.
ARTHUR. What?
SALLY. You'll end up selling it.
ARTHUR. Selling it?
SALLY. That's what will happen. It will kick around for a while, and you'll end up calling a furniture dealer. (*Annie comes out with a small glass of "orange juice" on a tray.*)
ARTHUR. I am absolutely amazed you'd say that.
SALLY. I don't want to fight, Arthur.
ARTHUR. Neither do I. Maybe we should defer the dining room. (*He starts for door, right.*)
SALLY. (*Following him.*) Maybe we should.
ANNIE. Good morning, sir.
FATHER. Good morning, Annie.
ARTHUR. Selling the dining room? Is that what you told Mother I'd do?
SALLY. (*Following him.*) I told her I'd give you the piano if I can have the dining room...
ARTHUR. I'll be lucky if I keep this spoon.
SALLY. I'll give you the piano and the coffee table if I can have the dining room. (*Arthur and Sally exit into the hall.*)
FATHER. Annie... (*Annie is almost to the kitchen door.*)
ANNIE. Yes sir...

10

FATHER. Did I find a seed in my orange juice yesterday morning?

ANNIE. I strained it, sir.

FATHER. I'm sure you did, Annie. Nonetheless I think I may have detected a small seed.

ANNIE. I'll strain it twice, sir.

FATHER. Seeds can wreak havoc with the digestion, Annie.

ANNIE. Yes, sir.

FATHER. They can take root. And grow.

ANNIE. Yes, sir. I'm sorry, sir. (*Annie goes out. Father drinks his orange juice carefully, and reads his newspaper. A little Girl sticks her head out through the dining room door.*)

GIRL. Daddy...

FATHER. Yes, good morning, Lizzie Boo.

GIRL. Dadddy, could Charlie and me—

FATHER. Charlie and I...

GIRL. ...Charlie and I come out and sit with you while you have breakfast?

FATHER. You certainly may, Lizzikins. I'd be delighted to have the pleasure of your company, provided—

GIRL. Yippee!

FATHER. I said, PROVIDED you sit quietly, without leaning back in your chairs, and don't fight or argue.

GIRL. (*Calling off.*) He says we *can!*

FATHER. I said you *may* sweetheart. (*The Girl comes out adoringly, followed by a Little Boy.*)

GIRL. (*Kissing her father.*) Good morning, Daddy.

BOY. (*Kissing him too.*) Morning, Dad. (*They settle into their seats. Annie brings out the Father's "breakfast."*)

ANNIE. Here's your cream, sir.

FATHER. Thank you Annie.

ANNIE. You're welcome, sir. (*Annie goes out. The children watch their father.*)

BOY. Dad...

FATHER. Hmmm?

11

BOY. When do we get to have fresh cream on our shreddded wheat?

GIRL. When you grow up, that's when.

FATHER. I'll tell you one thing. If there's a war, no one gets cream. If there's a war, we'll all have to settle for top of the bottle.

GIRL. Mother said she was thinking about having us eat dinner in here with you every night.

FATHER. Yes. Your mother and I are both thinking about that. And we're both looking forward to it. As soon as you children learn to sit up straight... (*They quickly do.*) then I see no reason why we shouldn't all have a pleasant meal together every evening.

BOY. Could we try it tonight, Dad? Could you give us a test?

FATHER. No, Charlie. Not tonight. Because tonight we're giving a small dinner party. But I hope very much you and Liz will come down and shake hands.

GIRL. I get so shy, Dad.

FATHER. Well you'll just have to learn, sweetie pie. Half of life is learning to meet people.

BOY. What's the other half, Dad? (*Pause. The Father fixes him with a steely gaze.*)

FATHER. Was that a crack?

BOY. No, Dad...

FATHER. That was a crack, wasn't it?

BOY. No, Dad. Really...

FATHER. That sounded very much like a smart-guy wisecrack to me. And people who make cracks like that don't normally eat in dining rooms.

BOY. I didn't mean it as a crack, Dad.

FATHER. Then we'll ignore it. We'll go on with out breakfast. (*Annie comes in.*)

ANNIE. (*To Girl.*) Your car's here, Lizzie. For school. (*Annie goes out.*)

GIRL. (*Jumping up.*) O.K.

FATHER. (*To Girl.*) Thank you, Annie.

GIRL. Thank you, Annie... (*Kisses Father.*) Goodbye, Daddy.

FATHER. Goodbye, darling. Don't be late. Say good morning

12

to the driver. Sit quietly in the car. Work hard. Run. Run. Goodbye. (*Girl goes off. Father returns to his paper. Pause. Boy sits watching his father.*)

BOY. Dad, can I read the funnies?

FATHER. Certainly. Certainly you may. (*He carefully extracts the second section and hands it to his son. Both read, the Son trying to imitate the Father in how he does it. Finally:*) This won't mean much to you, but the government is systematically ruining this country.

BOY. Miss Kelly told us about the government.

FATHER. Oh really. And who is Miss Kelly, pray tell?

BOY. She's my teacher.

FATHER. I don't remember any Miss Kelly.

BOY. She's new, Dad.

FATHER. I see. And what has she been telling you?

BOY. She said there's a depression going on.

FATHER. I see.

BOY. People all over the country are standing in line for bread.

FATHER. I see.

BOY. So the government has to step in and do something. (*Long pause. Then:*)

FATHER. Annie!

ANNIE. (*Coming out of kitchen.*) Yes, sir.

FATHER. I'd very much like some more coffee, please.

ANNIE. Yes, sir. (*Annie goes out.*)

FATHER. You tell Miss Kelly she's wrong.

BOY. Why?

FATHER. I'll tell you exactly why: if the government keeps on handing out money, no one will want to work. And if no one wants to work, there won't be anyone around to support such things as private schools. And if no one is supporting private schools, then Miss Kelly will be standing on the bread lines along with everyone else. You tell Miss Kelly that, if you please. Thank you, Annie. (*Annie comes in and pours coffee. Father returns to his paper. Annie has retreated to the kitchen. Boy reads his funnies for a moment. Then:*)

BOY. Dad...

13

FATHER. (*Reading*) Hmmm?

BOY. Could we leave a little earlier today?

FATHER. We'll leave when we always leave.

BOY. But I'm always late, Dad.

FATHER. Nonsense.

BOY. I am, Dad. Yesterday I had to walk into assembly while they were still singing the hymn.

FATHER. A minute or two late...

BOY. Everyone looked at me, Dad.

FATHER. You tell everyone to concentrate on that hymn.

BOY. I can't, Dad...

FATHER. It's that new stoplight on Richmond Avenue. It affects our timing.

BOY. It's not just the new stop light, Dad. Sometimes I come in when they're already doing arithmetic. Miss Kelly says I should learn to be punctual.

FATHER. (*Putting down paper.*) Miss Kelly again, eh?

BOY. She said if everyone is late, no one would learn any mathematics.

FATHER. Now you listen to me, Charlie. Miss Kelly may be an excellent teacher. Her factoring may be flawless, her geography beyond question. But Miss Kelly does not teach us politics. Nor does she teach us how to run our lives. She is not going to tell you, or me, to leave in the middle of a pleasant breakfast, and get caught in the bulk of the morning traffic, just so that you can arrive in time for a silly hymn. Long after you've forgotten that hymn, long after you've forgotten how to factor, long after you've forgotten Miss Kelly, you will remember these pleasant breakfasts around this dining room table. (*Mother glides into the room from the R.*) And here is your mother to prove it.

MOTHER. (*Kissing Father.*) Good morning, dear. (*Kissing Charlie.*) Good morning, Charlie.

FATHER. (*Remaining seated.*) I know people who leap to their feet when a beautiful woman enters the room. (*Charlie jumps up.*)

14

MOTHER. Oh that's all right, dear.

FATHER. I also know people who rush to push in their mother's chair. *(Charlie does so.)*

MOTHER. Thank you, dear.

FATHER. And finally, I know people who are quick to give their mother the second section of the morning paper.

CHARLIE. Oh! Here, Mum.

MOTHER. Thank you, dear.

FATHER. Now Charlie: take a moment, if you would, just to look at your lovely mother, bathed in the morning sunlight, and reflected in the dining room table.

MOTHER. Oh Russell... *(Charlie looks at his mother.)*

FATHER. Look at her, Charlie, and then ask yourself carefully: Which is worth our ultimate attention? Your Mother? Or Miss Kelly?

MOTHER. Who is Miss Kelly?

FATHER. Never mind, dear. Which, Charlie?

CHARLIE. My Mother.

FATHER. Good, Charlie. Fine. *(He gets up; taking his section of the paper.)* And now, I think you and I should make a trip upstairs before we say goodbye, and are on our way. *(Mother smiles sweetly. Charlie gives his Mother a kiss. Father and Son leave the room. Annie enters, carrying coffee server.)*

MOTHER. Good morning, Annie.

ANNIE. Good morning, Mrs.

MOTHER. Tell Irma I'll have poached eggs this morning, please, Annie.

ANNIE. Yes, Mrs. *(Annie goes out. Mother sits sipping coffee, reading her section of the paper. A Youngish Woman— call her Ellie— comes out of the kitchen. Her arms are stacked with a small portable typewriter, papers, several books and notebooks. She finds a place at the table and begins to spread things out around her. Mother pays no attention to her. A Man called Howard, carrying a briefcase, appears at R.)*

HOWARD. Hey!

ELLIE. Ooooops. I thought you had gone.

HOWARD. I forgot my briefcase... What's going on?

ELLIE. I have to get this term paper done.

HOWARD. In here?

ELLIE. Where else.

HOWARD. You're going to *type?*

ELLIE. Of course I'm going to type.

HOWARD. In here? At that table?

ELLIE. Why not?

HOWARD. You're going to sit there, banging a typewriter on my family's dining room *table?*

ELLIE. Why not?

HOWARD. Because it wasn't designed for it, that's why!

ELLIE. (*Sighing*) Oh, Howard...

HOWARD. Lucky I came back. Next thing you know, you'll be feeding the dog off our Lowestoft china.

ELLIE. It's got rubber pads under it. I checked. (*Gets up, goes to sideboard.*) And I'll get something else, if you want. (*She takes out a couple of place mats.*)

HOWARD. You're not going to use those place mats?

ELLIE. I thought I would. Yes.

HOWARD. Those are good place mats.

ELLIE. We haven't used them in ten years.

HOWARD. Those are extremely good place mats, Ellie. Mother got those in Italy.

ELLIE. All *right.* (*She puts the place mats back in the sideboard rummages around finds a couple of hot pads. He watches her carefully.*) I'll use these, then. Mind if I use these? We put pots on them. We can certainly put a typewriter. (*She carries them to the table, puts them under the typewriter, continues to get things set up. Howard watches her. Meanwhile, Mother, impatient for her poached eggs, puts down her paper and rings a little silver bell on the table in front of her. Annie comes out of the kitchen.*)

ANNIE. Yes, Mrs?

MOTHER. I wonder if anything might have happened to my poached eggs, Annie.

ANNIE. Irma's cooking two more, Mrs.

MOTHER. Two more?

16

ANNIE. The first ones slid off the plate while she was buttering the toast.

MOTHER. (*Standing up.*) Is she drinking again, Annie?

ANNIE. No, Mrs.

MOTHER. Tell me the truth.

ANNIE. I don't think so, Mrs.

MOTHER. I'd better go see...A simple question of two poached eggs. (*She starts for the kitchen.*) Honestly, Annie, sometimes I think it's almost better if we just do things our*selves*.

ANNIE. Yes, Mrs. (*Mother goes out into the kitchen; Annie clears the Mother's and Father's places, leaving a glass and plate for the next scene. Annie exits.*)

ELLIE. (*To Howard, who is standing at the doorway, still watching.*) Don't you have a plane to catch? It's kind of hard to work when your husband is hovering over you, like a helicopter.

HOWARD. Well it's kind of hard to leave when your wife is systematically mutilating the dining room table.

ELLIE. I'll be careful, Howard. I swear. Now goodbye. (*She begins to hunt and peck on the typewriter. Howard starts out, then wheels on her.*)

HOWARD. Couldn't you *please* work somewhere else?

ELLIE. I'd like to know where, please.

HOWARD. What's wrong with the kitchen table?

ELLIE. It doesn't work, Howard. Last time the kids got peanut butter all over my footnotes.

HOWARD. I'll set up the bridge table in the living room.

ELLIE. I'd just have to move whenever you and the boys wanted to watch a football game.

HOWARD. You mean, you're going to leave all that stuff *there*?

ELLIE. I thought I would. Yes.

HOWARD. All that shit? All over the dining room?

ELLIE. It's a term paper, Howard. It's crucial for my degree.

HOWARD. You mean you're going to commandeer the *dining* room for the rest of the *term*?

ELLIE. It just sits here, Howard. It's never used.

HOWARD. What if we want to give a dinner party?

ELLIE. Since when have we given a dinner party?

HOWARD. What if we want to have a few people *over*, for Chrissake?

ELLIE. We can eat in the kitchen.

HOWARD. Oh Jesus.

ELLIE. Everybody does these days.

HOWARD. That doesn't make it right.

ELLIE. Let me get this done, Howard! Let me get a good grade, and my Master's degree and a good job, so I can be *out* of here every day!

HOWARD. Fine! What the hell! Then why don't I turn it into a *tool* room, every night? (*He storms out. Ellie doggedly returns to her work, angrily hunting and pecking on the typewriter. Grace enters from R. She sits D.L., and begins to work on her grocery list. Carolyn, a girl of fourteen, enters sleepily a moment later.*)

CAROLYN. Why did you tell Mildred to wake me up, Mother?

GRACE. Let me just finish this grocery list.

CAROLYN. I mean it's Saturday, Mother.

GRACE. (*Finishing the list with a flourish.*) Sshh...There. (*Puts down the list.*) I know it's Saturday, darling, and I apologize. But something has come up, and I want you to make a little decision.

CAROLYN. What decision?

GRACE. Start your breakfast, dear. No one can think on an empty stomach. (*Carolyn sits at the table.*) Now. Guess who telephoned this morning?

CAROLYN. Who?

GRACE. Your Aunt Martha.

CAROLYN. Oh I love her.

GRACE. So do I. But the poor thing hasn't got enough to do, so she was on the telephone at the crack of dawn.

CAROLYN. What did she want?

GRACE. Well now here's the thing: she's got an extra ticket for the theatre tonight, and she wants you to join her.

CAROLYN. Sure!

GRACE. Now wait till I've finished, dear. I told her it was

18

your decision, of course, but I thought you had other plans.

CAROLYN. What other plans?

GRACE. Now think, darling. Isn't there something rather special going on in your life this evening? (*Pause.*)

CAROLYN. Oh.

GRACE. Am I right, or am I right.

CAROLYN. (*Grimly.*) Dancing school.

ELLIE. Shit. (*She begins to gather up her materials.*)

GRACE. Not dancing school, sweetheart. The first session of the Junior Assemblies. Which are a big step beyond dancing school.

ELLIE. I can't work in this place! It's like a tomb! (*She goes out into the kitchen.*)

GRACE. I told Aunt Martha you'd call her right back, so she could drum up someone else.

CAROLYN. I thought it was my decision.

GRACE. It is, sweetheart. Of course.

CAROLYN. Then I'd like to see a play with Aunt Martha. (*Pause.*)

GRACE. Carolyn, I wonder if you're being just a little impulsive this morning. You don't even know what the play is.

CAROLYN. What is it, then?

GRACE. Well it happens to be a very talky play called *Saint Joan*.

CAROLYN. Oh we read that in school! I want to go all the more!

GRACE. It's the road company, sweetheart. It doesn't even have Katherine Cornell.

CAROLYN. I'd still like to go.

GRACE. To some endless play? With your maiden aunt?

CAROLYN. She's my favorite person.

GRACE. Well then go, if it's that important to you.

CAROLYN. (*Getting up.*) I'll call her right now. (*She starts for the door.*)

GRACE. Carolyn... (*Carolyn stops.*) You realize, of course, that on the first Junior Assembly, everyone gets acquainted.

19

CAROLYN. Really?

GRACE. Oh heavens yes. It starts the whole thing off on the right foot.

CAROLYN. I didn't know that.

GRACE. Oh yes. It's like the first day of school. Once you miss, you never catch up.

CAROLYN. Oh gosh.

GRACE. You see? You see why we shouldn't make hasty decisions. (*Pause.*)

CAROLYN. Then maybe I won't go at all.

GRACE. What do you mean?

CAROLYN. Maybe I'll skip all the Junior Assemblies.

GRACE. Oh Carolyn.

CAROLYN. I don't like dancing school anyway.

GRACE. Don't be silly.

CAROLYN. I don't. I've never liked it. I'm bigger than half the boys, and I never know what to say, and I'm a terrible dancer. Last year I spent half the time in the ladies room.

GRACE. That's nonsense.

CAROLYN. It's true, Mother. I hate dancing school. I don't know why I have to go. Saint Joan wouldn't go to dancing school in a million years!

GRACE. Yes, and look what happened to Saint Joan!

CAROLYN. I don't care. I've made up my mind. (*Pause.*)

GRACE. Your Aunt Martha seems to have caused a little trouble around here this morning.

CAROLYN. Maybe.

GRACE. Your Aunt Martha seems to have opened up a whole can of worms.

CAROLYN. I'm glad she did.

GRACE. All right. And how do you propose to spend your other Saturday nights? I mean, when there's no Aunt Martha. And no Saint Joan? And all your friends are having the time of their life at Junior Assemblies?

CAROLYN. I'll do something.

GRACE. Such as what? Hanging around here? Listening to that stupid Hit Parade? Bothering the maids when we're planning to have a party? (*Aggie, a Maid, comes out of the kitchen, sits at the table, begins to polish some flat silver with a silver cloth.*)

CAROLYN. I'll do *some*thing, Mother.

GRACE. (*Picking up Carolyn's breakfast dishes.*) Well you're obviously not old enough to make an intelligent decision.

CAROLYN. I knew you wouldn't let me decide.

GRACE. (*Wheeling on her.*) All right, then! Decide!

CAROLYN. I'd like to—

GRACE. But let me tell you a very short story before you do. About your dear Aunt Martha. Who also made a little decision when she was about your age. She decided—if you breathe a word of this, I'll strangle you—she decided she was in love with her riding master. And so she threw everything up, and ran off with him. To Taos, New Mexico. Where your father had to track her down and drag her back. But it was too late, Carolyn! She had been...overstimulated. And from then on in, she refused to join the workday world. Now there it is. In a nutshell. So think about it, while I'm ordering the groceries. And decide. (*She goes out L., carrying Carolyn's glass and plate. Aggie polishes the silver. Carolyn sits and thinks. She decides.*)

CAROLYN. I've decided, Mother.

GRACE'S VOICE. (*From the kitchen.*) Good. I hope you've come to your senses.

CAROLYN. (*Getting up.*) I've decided to talk to Aunt Martha. (*She goes out.*)

GRACE. (*Bursting through the kitchen door.*) You've got a dentist appointment, Carolyn! You've got riding lessons at noon—no, no, we'll skip the riding lessons, but—Carolyn! Carolyn! (*She rushes out through the hall as Michael comes in through the kitchen. He is about twelve.*)

MICHAEL. (*Sneaking up on her.*) Boo!

AGGIE. Michael! You scared me out of my skin!

MICHAEL. I wanted to. (*Pause. He comes a little more into the room. Aggie returns to her polishing.*)

AGGIE. Your mother said you was sick this morning.

MICHAEL. I was. I am.

21

AGGIE. So sick you couldn't go to school.

MICHAEL. I *am,* Aggie! I upchucked! Twice!

AGGIE. Then you get right straight back to bed. (*He doesn't.*)

MICHAEL. How come you didn't do my room yet?

AGGIE. Because I thought you was sleeping.

MICHAEL. I've just been *lying* there, Ag. Waiting.

AGGIE. Well I got more to do now, since Ida left. I got the silver, and the downstairs lavatory, and all the beds besides. (*He comes farther in.*)

MICHAEL. My mother says you want to leave us. (*She polishes.*)

AGGIE. When did she say that?

MICHAEL. Last Thursday. On your day off. When she was cooking dinner. She said now there's a war, you're looking for a job with more money. (*Aggie polishes.*) Is that true, Ag?

AGGIE. Maybe.

MICHAEL. Money isn't everything, Aggie.

AGGIE. Listen to him now.

MICHAEL. You can be rich as a king and still be miserable. Look at my Uncle Paul. He's rich as Croesus and yet he's drinking himself into oblivion.

AGGIE. What do you know about all that?

MICHAEL. I know a lot. I eat dinner here in the dining room now. I listen. And I know that my Uncle Paul is drinking himself into oblivion. And Mrs. Williams has a tipped uterus.

AGGIE. Here now. You stop that talk.

MICHAEL. Well, it's *true,* Ag. And it proves that money isn't everything. So you don't have to leave us. (*Pause. She works. He drifts around the table.*)

AGGIE. It's not just the money, darlin'.

MICHAEL. Then *what,* Ag? (*No answer.*) Don't you like us any more?

AGGIE. Oh, Michael...

MICHAEL. Don't you like our family?

AGGIE. Oh, Mikey...

22

MICHAEL. Are you still mad at me for peeking at you in the bathtub?

AGGIE. That's enough now.

MICHAEL. Then what *is* it, Ag? How come you're just leaving? (*Pause.*)

AGGIE. Because I don't... (*Pause.*) I don't want to do domestic service no more.

MICHAEL. Why?

AGGIE. Because I don't like it no more, Mike. (*He thinks.*)

MICHAEL. That's because Ida left and you have too much to do, Ag.

AGGIE. No darlin'...

MICHAEL. (*Sitting down near her.*) I'll help you, Ag. I swear! I'll make my own bed, and pick up my towel. I'll try to be much more careful when I pee!

AGGIE. (*Laughing.*) Lord love you, lad.

MICHAEL. No, no, really. I will. And I'll tell my parents not to have so many dinner parties, Ag. I'll tell them to give you more time off. I'll tell them to give you all day Sunday.

AGGIE. No, darlin'. No.

MICHAEL. I'm *serious*, Ag.

AGGIE. I know, darlin'! I know. (*Two Men come in from R.; an Architect and a prospective Buyer.*)

ARCHITECT. O.K. Let's measure it out then. (*The Architect has a large reel tape-measure to and a roll of blueprints. They begin to measure the room systematically, the Architect reading the figures and recording them in a small notebook, the Buyer holding the end of the tape. They first measure the D. length.*)

MICHAEL. When will you be going then, Ag?

AGGIE. As soon as your mother finds someone else.

MICHAEL. She can't *find* anyone, Aggie.

AGGIE. She will, she will.

MICHAEL. She says she *can't*. They keep showing up with dirty fingernails and dyed hair!

ARCHITECT. (*Reading measurements, writing them down.*)

23

Twenty-two feet, six inches.

BUYER. Fine room.

ARCHITECT. Big room.

MICHAEL. So you *got* to stay, Ag. You can't just leave people in the *lurch*.

BUYER. Look at these French doors.

ARCHITECT. I'm looking. I'm also thinking. About heat loss. (*They measure more.*)

AGGIE. I'll stay till you go away for the summer.

ARCHITECT. (*Measuring width of "French doors."*) Eight feet two inches. (*Michael gets up and comes D., looks out through the French doors, as the Architect goes U., to record his notes on the sideboard.*)

MICHAEL. You gonna get married, aren't you, Ag?

AGGIE. Maybe.

MICHAEL. That guy you told me about from church?

AGGIE. Maybe.

MICHAEL. You gonna have children? (*Aggie laughs.*) You will. I know you will. You'll have a boy of your own.

ARCHITECT. Hold it tight now.

MICHAEL. Will you come back to see us?

AGGIE. Oh my yes.

MICHAEL. You won't, Ag.

AGGIE. I will surely.

MICHAEL. You'll never come back, Ag. I'll never see you again! Ever!

ARCHITECT. (*Now measuring the width.*) Twelve feet four inches...

AGGIE. (*Holding out her arms.*) Come here, Mike.

MICHAEL. No.

AGGIE. Come here and give Aggie a big hug!

MICHAEL. No. Why should I? No.

AGGIE. Just a squeeze, for old time's sake!

MICHAEL. No! (*Squaring his shoulders.*) Go hug your own kids, Agnes. I've got work to do. I've got a whole stack of homework to do. I'm missing a whole day of school. (*He runs out of the room.*)

AGGIE. Michael! (*She resumes polishing the last few pieces of silver.*)

ARCHITECT. (*Reeling in his tape with professional zeal.*) O.K. There's your dining room, Doctor.

BUYER. (*Who is a psychiatrist.*) There it is.

ARCHITECT. Big room...light room...commodious room...

PSYCHIATRIST. One of the reasons we bought the house.

ARCHITECT. And one of the reasons we should consider breaking it up.

PSYCHIATRIST. Breaking it up?

ARCHITECT. Now bear with me: What say we turn this room into an office for you, and a waiting room for your patients?

PSYCHIATRIST. I thought we planned to open up those maid's rooms on the third floor.

ARCHITECT. Hold on. Relax. (*He begins to spread a large blueprint out on the table, anchoring its corners with his tape measure and centerpiece. Aggie has finished polishing by now. She gathers up her silver and polishing stuff and leaves.*) The patient trusts the psychiatrist, doesn't he? Why can't the psychiatrist trust the architect? (*He begins to sketch on the blueprint, with a grease pencil.*) Now here's the ground plan of your house. Here's what you're stuck with, for the moment, and here, with these approximate dimensions, is your dining room.

PSYCHIATRIST. I see.

ARCHITECT. (*Drawing with his grease pencil.*) Now suppose ...just suppose...we started with a clean slate. Suppose we open this up here, slam a beam in here, break through here and here, blast out this, throw out that, and what do we have?

PSYCHIATRIST. I'm not quite sure.

ARCHITECT. Well we don't have a dining room anymore. That's what we don't have.

PSYCHIATRIST. But where would we eat?

ARCHITECT. Here. Right here. Look. I'm putting in an eating area. Here's the fridge, the cooking units, Cuisinart, butcher-block table, chrome chairs. See? Look at the space. The flow. Wife cooks, kids set the table, you stack the dishes. All right

25

here. Democracy at work. In your own home.

PSYCHIATRIST. Hmm.

ARCHITECT. Now, let's review your day. You come down to breakfast, everybody's fixing his or her own thing. (*He goes out through the hall, reappears through the kitchen door.*) Eggs, cornflakes, pop-tarts, whatever. You eat, chat, read the paper, say goodbye, come in here to go to work, Do you have a nurse or a receptionist?

PSYCHIATRIST. No, no. I'm just a humble shrink.

ARCHITECT. (*Beginning to move around the room.*) Well, you come in here to the reception room, maybe adjust the magazines on a table, here, maybe add your newspaper to the pile, then you go through a sound-proof door into your office. You turn on your stereo-console here, maybe select a book form a wall-unit here, and then settle behind your desk module here. You read, you listen to music. Soon—buzz—a patient arrives. You turn off the music, put aside your book, and buzz him in through the sound-proof doors. He flops on the couch here, (*He creates the couch with two U. chairs.*) tells you his dream, you look out the window here, he leaves, you write him up, buzz in the next. Soon it's time for lunch. You go in here, have lunch with the wife, or one of the kids, and maybe stroll back in here for a nap. More buzzes, more patients, and soon it's time for a good easy cooperative supper with your family.

PSYCHIATRIST. But not in the dining room.

ARCHITECT. No. Not in the dining room.

PSYCHIATRIST. This room has such resonance.

ARCHITECT. So does a church. That doesn't mean we have to live in it.

PSYCHIATRIST. Mmm.

ARCHITECT. Look, I know whereof I speak: I grew up in a room like this.

PSYCHIATRIST. Oh, yes?

ARCHITECT. Oh sure. This is home turf to me.

PSYCHIATRIST. Really.

ARCHITECT. Oh God yes. My father sat in a chair just like that...

26

PSYCHIATRIST. (*Beginning to look out the window.*) Mmmm.

ARCHITECT. And my mother sat here. And my sister here. And I sat right here. (*He sits.*) Oh, it all comes back . . .

PSYCHIATRIST. (*After a pause.*) Do you want to tell me about it?

ARCHITECT. It was torture, that's all. Those endless meals, waiting to begin, waiting for the dessert, waiting to be excused so they couldn't lean on you any more.

PSYCHIATRIST. (*Almost by rote.*) Was it that bad?

ARCHITECT. Man, it was brutal. I remember one time I came to the table without washing my hands, and my father—(*He stops.*)

PSYCHIATRIST. Go on.

ARCHITECT. (*Snapping out of it, getting up.*) Never mind. The point is, Doctor, it's time to get rid of this room. (*He begins to roll up his plans.*) Tell you frankly, I'm not interested in screwing around with any more maid's rooms. I can do that in my sleep. (*Peggy comes out of the kitchen, carrying a large tray, loaded with paper plates, napkins, hats and favors for a children's birthday party. She begins to set the table.*) What I want is the chance to get in here, so I can open up your whole ground floor! Now what do you say?

PSYCHIATRIST. I'll have to think about it.

ARCHITECT. O.K. Fine. Take your time. (*He starts out.*) Tell you what. I'll send you my bill for the work I've done so far.

PSYCHIATRIST. Good. And I'll send you mine. (*They are out. Peggy, meanwhile, is finishing setting the birthday table. She surveys it, then goes to the doorway, R., and calls off.*)

PEGGY. All right, Children! We're ready! (*She is almost bowled over by a moiling, shrieking mob of children coming in to celebrate the birthday party. They scream, yell, scramble over chairs, grab for favors, wrestle, whatever. Peggy claps her hands frantically.*) Children, children, CHILDREN! (*They subside a little.*) This is a *dining* room! This is *not* the monkey house at the zoo! (*They all start imitating monkeys. Peggy shouts them down.*) All right then. I'll just have to tell Roberta in the kitchen to put away all the ice cream and cake. (*The noice subsides. There is silence.*) Good. That's much better. Now I want everyone to leave the table...quietly, QUIETLY... (*The children begin to leave.*) And go into the hall, and then come back in here in the right way. That's it. Go out. Turn around. And come in. Come in as if you were your mummies and daddies coming into a lovely dinner party. (*Children come back in much more decorously, unconsciously parodying their parents.*) No, no. Let Winkie go first, since it's her birthday and she's the hostess...That's it. Good. Good. You sit at the head of the table, Winkie...Good...No, no, Billy, you sit next to Winkie...It should be boy-girl, boy-girl...That's it. Yes. Very good. (*Children are making a concerted effort to be genteel, though there are occasional subversive pokings, hitting, and gigglings.*) Now what do we do with our napkins?...Yes. Exactly. We unfold them and tuck them under our chins...And then we put on our party hats...

A LITTLE BOY. (*Named Brewster.*) Can the boys wear their hats in the house?

PEGGY. Yes they can, Brewster, because this is a special occasion. And sometimes on special occasions, the rules can change. (*Children explode. Ray! Yippee! Peggy has to shout them down.*) I said *some*times. And I meant some of the rules.

ANOTHER LITTLE BOY. (*Named Billy: pointing toward the hall.*) There's my Daddy.

PEGGY. (*Quickly.*) Where, Billy? (*Ted comes On from the hall; she tries to be casual.*) Oh. Hi.

TED. Hi. (*Waves to son.*) Hi, Bill. (*Party activity continues, the children opening favors. Peggy and Ted move D. to get away from the noise.*)

PEGGY. What brings you here?

TED. Have to pick up Bill.

PEGGY. I thought Judy was picking him up.

TED. She asked me to.

PEGGY. You're a little early. We haven't even had our cake.

TED. She told me to be early. (*A Little Girl calls from the table.*)

A LITTLE GIRL. (*Named Sandra: fussing with favor.*) I can't get mine to work.
PEGGY. Help her, Brewster. Little boys are supposed to help little girls.
TED. Where's Frank?
PEGGY. Playing golf. Where else?
TED. On Winkie's birthday?
PEGGY. Don't get me started. Please. (*Winkie calls from the head of the table.*)
WINKIE. Can we have the ice cream now, please.
PEGGY. In a minute, dear. Be patient. Then you'll have something to look forward to. (*The children whisperingly begin to count to sixty.*)
TED. Judy must have known he'd be playing golf.
PEGGY. Judy knows everything.
TED. She knows about us, at least.
PEGGY. About us? How?
TED. She said she could tell by the way we behaved.
PEGGY. Behaved? Where?
TED. At the Bramwell's dinner party.
PEGGY. We hardly spoke to each other.
TED. That's how she could tell. (*The children's counting has turned into a chant*: "We want ice cream! We want ice cream!")
PEGGY. They want ice cream. (*She starts for the kitchen.*)
TED. (*Holding her arm.*) She says she'll fight it, tooth and nail.
PEGGY. Fight *what*? We haven't done anything.
TED. She wants to nip it in the bud.
CHILDREN. Ice cream! Ice cream!
PEGGY. All right, children. You win. (*Cheers from children.*) Now Roberta is very busy in the kitchen because she also has a dinner party tonight. So who would like to help bring things out? (*Hands up, squeals*: "Me! Me!") All right. Tell you what. Billy, you get the ice cream, and Sandra, you bring out the cake! ("*Ray! Yippee!*") Careful, careful! Walk, don't run! And be polite to Roberta because she's working very hard. And

29

Brewster and Winkie, you'll have other responsibilities! *(Sandra and Billy go out into the kitchen.)* For instance, Brewster: when Billy and Sandra reappear through that door, what will you do? *(Long pause.)*

BREWSTER. Sing the song.

PEGGY. Good, Brewster. Now be very quiet, and watch that door, and as soon as they come out, start singing. *(The children watch the door. Peggy hurries back to Ted.)* So what do we do?

TED. She says she's thinking of telling her father about us.

PEGGY. Her *father?*

TED. He'd fire me. Immediately.

PEGGY. What if he did?

TED. I'd be out of a job, Peggy.

PEGGY. You could get another.

TED. Where? Doing what? *(The dining room door opens. Billy and Sandra come out carefully carrying a cake platter and an ice cream bowl. Everyone starts singing a birthday song, probably out of tune. Peggy helps them along. Billy puts the cake down in front of Winkie, who takes a deep breath to blow out the candles.)*

PEGGY. No, no, sweetheart. Wait. Always wait. Before you blow out the candles, you have to make a wish. And Mummy has to make a wish. See? Mummy is putting her wedding ring around one of the candles. Now we both close our eyes and make a wish.

WINKIE. I wish I could have—

PEGGY. No, no. Don't tell. Never tell a wish. If you do, it won't come true. All right. Now blow. *(Winkie blows out "the candles." The children cheer.)* Now Winkie, would you cut the cake and give everyone a piece, please. And Brewster, you pass the ice cream. *(The children organize their food as Peggy joins Ted D. There is a kind of cooing hum of children eating which punctuates their dialogue.)*

TED. What did you wish for?

PEGGY. Won't tell.

TED. Do you think it will come true?

PEGGY. No. (*Pause.*)

TED. She'd make it so messy. For everyone.

PEGGY. Judy.

TED. She'd make it impossible.

PEGGY. So would Frank.

TED. I thought he didn't care.

PEGGY. He'd care if it were messy. (*Pause.*)

TED. We could leave town.

PEGGY. And go where?

TED. Wherever I find another job.

PEGGY. Yes...

TED. I've got an uncle in Syracuse.

PEGGY. Syracuse?

TED. We could live there.

PEGGY. Is it nice? Syracuse?

TED. I think it's on some lake.

PEGGY. Syracuse...

TED. You'd have Winkie. I'd get Bill in the summer.

PEGGY. In Syracuse.

TED. At least we'd be free. (*They look at their children.*)

PEGGY. Winkie, wipe your mouth, please. (*She goes to Winkie.*)

TED. Billy.

BILLY. What?

TED. Would you come here a minute, please? (*Billy does. Ted takes him aside.*) Do you have to go the bathroom?

BILLY. No.

TED. Then don't do that, please.

BILLY. Don't do what?

TED. You know what. Now go back and enjoy the party. (*Billy returns to his seat. Ted rejoins Peggy.*) Sorry.

PEGGY. I grew up here.

TED. Who didn't?

PEGGY. To just pick up stakes...

31

TED. I know.

PEGGY. I mean, this is where I *live*.

TED. Me, too. (*Touching her.*) We'll just have to behave ourselves, then.

PEGGY. Oh Ted...

TED. Be good little children.

PEGGY. Oh I can't stand it. (*She takes his hand and presses it furtively to her lips.*)

TED. And if we're seated next to each other, we'll have to make a conscious effort.

PEGGY. Oh we won't be seated next to each other. Judy will see to that.

TED. For a while, any way.

PEGGY. For quite a while. (*The children are getting noisy. Winkie comes up.*)

WINKIE. Everyone's finished, Mummy.

PEGGY. Thank you, sweetheart.

WINKIE. And here's your ring. From the cake.

PEGGY. Good for you, darling! I forgot all about it! (*She puts the ring back on.*)

TED. Time to go, then?

PEGGY. I've planned some games.

TED. Want me to stay?

PEGGY. It would help.

TED. Then I'll stay.

PEGGY. (*To children.*) Into the living room now, children. For some games.

BREWSTER. What games?

PEGGY. Oh all kinds of games! Blind Man's Bluff. Pin the Tail on the Donkey...

CHILDREN. Yippee! Yay! (*The children run noisily Off. Peggy begins putting the mess back onto the tray.*)

TED. I'll get them started.

PEGGY. Would you? While I propitiate Roberta.

TED. I'll be the donkey.

PEGGY. Oh stop.

TED. I'll be the ass.

PEGGY. Stop or I'll scream. (*He is about to kiss her, over the tray, when Winkie appears at the door. They break away.*)

WINKIE. Come *on*, Mummy! We're waiting!

PEGGY. We're coming, dear. (*Winkie disappears into the hall. Ted and Peggy go off different ways as a Grandfather enters from the hall. He is about eighty. He sits at the head of the table, as a maid, Dora comes out of the kitchen and begins to set a place in front of him. After a moment, his grandson Nick breathlessly appears in the doorway from the hall. He is about thirteen or fourteen.*)

NICK. (*Panting, frightened.*) Grampa?

GRANDFATHER. (*Looking up.*) Which one are you?

NICK. I'm Nick, Gramp.

GRANDFATHER. And what do you want?

NICK. To have lunch with you, Gramp.

GRANDFATHER. Then you're late.

NICK. I went down to the club.

GRANDFATHER. Who said I'd be at the club?

NICK. My parents. My parents said you always eat there.

GRANDFATHER. Lately I've been coming home.

NICK. Yes, sir.

GRANDFATHER. Don't know half the people at the club any more. Rather be here. At my own table. Dora takes care of me, don't you Dora?

DORA. Yes, sir.

GRANDFATHER. (*To Nick.*) Well you tracked me down, anyway. That shows some enterprise. (*Indicates a place.*) Bring him some lunch, Dora.

DORA. Yes, sir. (*She goes out.*)

NICK. (*Sitting opposite him at the other end of the table.*) Thank you, Gramp.

GRANDFATHER. So you're Nick, eh?

NICK. Yes. I am.

GRANDFATHER. You the one who wants to go to Europe this summer?

NICK. No, that's Mary. That's my cousin.

GRANDFATHER. You the one who wants the automobile? Says he can't go to college without an automobile?

NICK. No, that's my brother Tony, Gramp.

GRANDFATHER. What do you want then?

NICK. Oh I don't really want ...

GRANDFATHER. Everyone who sits down with me wants something. Usually it's money. Do you want money?

NICK. Yes, sir.

GRANDFATHER. For what?

NICK. My education, Gramp.

GRANDFATHER. Education, eh? That's a good thing. Or can be. Doesn't have to be. Can be a bad thing. Where do you want to be educated?

NICK. Saint Luke's School, in Litchfield, Connecticut.

GRANDFATHER. Never heard of it.

NICK. It's an excellent boarding school for boys.

GRANDFATHER. Is it Catholic?

NICK. I don't think so, Gramp.

GRANDFATHER. Sounds Catholic to me.

NICK. I think it's high Episcopalian, Gramp.

GRANDFATHER. Then it's expensive.

NICK. My parents think it's a first-rate school, Gramp.

GRANDFATHER. Ah. Your parents think ...

NICK. They've discussed all the boarding schools, and decided that this is the best.

GRANDFATHER. They decided, eh?

NICK. Yes, sir.

GRANDFATHER. And then they decided you should get your grandfather to pay for it.

NICK. Yes, sir. (*Dora has returned, and set a place mat and a plate for Nick.*)

GRANDFATHER. Another one leaving the nest, Dora.

DORA. Yes, sir. (*She waits by the sideboard.*)

GRANDFATHER. And taking a piece of the nest egg.

DORA. Yes, sir. (*Pause.*)

GRANDFATHER. Why don't you stay home?

34

NICK. Me?

GRANDFATHER. You.

NICK. Oh. Because I want to broaden myself.

GRANDFATHER. You want to what?

NICK. I want to broaden my horizons. My horizons need broadening.

GRANDFATHER. I see.

NICK. And I'll meet interesting new friends.

GRANDFATHER. Don't you have any interesting friends here?

NICK. Oh sure, Gramp.

GRANDFATHER. I do. I have interesting friends right here. I know a man who makes boats in his basement.

NICK. But...

GRANDFATHER. I know a man who plays golf with his wife.

NICK. But I'll meet different types, Gramp. From all over the country. New York...California...

GRANDFATHER. Why would you want to meet anyone from New York?

NICK. Well they're more sophisticated, Gramp. They'll buff me up.

GRANDFATHER. They'll what?

NICK. My mother says I need buffing up.

GRANDFATHER. Do you think he needs buffing up, Dora?

DORA. No, sir.

GRANDFATHER. (*To Nick.*) Dora doesn't think you need buffing up. I don't think you need buffing up. You'll have to give us better reasons.

NICK. Um. Well. They have advanced Latin there...

GRANDFATHER. I see. And?

NICK. And an indoor hockey rink.

GRANDFATHER. Yes. And?

NICK. And beautiful grounds and surroundings.

GRANDFATHER. Don't we? Don't we have beautiful surroundings? Why do we have to go away to have beautiful surroundings?

NICK. I don't know, Gramp. All I know is everyone's going

away these days.

GRANDFATHER. Everyone's going away? Hear that, Dora? Everyone's going away.

NICK. *(Desperately.)* An awful lot of people are going away! *(Pause.)*

GRANDFATHER. I didn't go away.

NICK. I know, Gramp.

GRANDFATHER. Didn't even go to Country Day. Went to the old P.S. 36 down on Huron Street.

NICK. Yes, Gramp.

GRANDFATHER. Didn't finish, either. Father died, and I had to go to work. Had to support my mother.

NICK. I know that, Gramp.

GRANDFATHER. My father didn't go to school at all. Learned Greek at the plow.

NICK. You told us, Gramp.

GRANDFATHER. Yes well I didn't do too badly. Without a high Episcopal boarding school, and an indoor hockey rink.

NICK. But you're a self-made man, Gramp.

GRANDFATHER. Oh is that what I am? And what are you? Don't you want to be self-made? Or do you want other people to make you? Hmmm? Hmmm? What've you got to say to that?

NICK. *(Squashed.)* I don't know ...

GRANDFATHER. Everyone wants to go away. Me? I went away twice. Took two vacations in my life. First vacation, took a week off from work to marry your grandmother. Went to Hot Springs, Virginia. Bought this table. Second vacation: Europe. 1928. Again with your grandmother. Hated the place. Knew I would. Miserable meals. Took a trunkload of shredded wheat along. Came back when it ran out. Back to this table. *(Pause.)* They're all leaving us, Dora. Scattering like birds.

DORA. Yes, sir.

GRANDFATHER. We're small potatoes these days.

DORA. Yes, sir.

GRANDFATHER. This one wants to go to one of those fancy

New England boarding schools. He wants to play ice hockey indoors with that crowd from Long Island and Philadelphia. He'll come home talking with marbles in his mouth. We won't understand a word, Dora.

DORA. Yes, sir.

GRANDFATHER. And we won't see much of him, Dora. He'll go visiting in New York and Baltimore. He'll drink liquor in the afternoon and get mixed up with women who wear lipstick and trousers and whose only thought is the next dance. And he wants me to pay for it all. Am I right?

NICK. No, Gramp! No I don't! I don't want to go! Really! I never wanted to go! I want to stay home with all of you!

GRANDFATHER. Finish your greens. They're good for your lower intestine. (*They eat silently. From L. a man named Paul enters. He's in his mid-thirties and wears a sweater. He starts carefully examining the dining room chairs along the left wall, one by one, turning them upside down, testing their strength. Finally; with a sigh; to Nick.*) No. You go. You've got to go. I'll send you to Saint Whoozie's and Betsy to Miss Whatsie's and young Andy to whatever-it's-called. And Mary can go to Europe this summer, and Tony can have a car, and it's all fine and dandy. (*He gets slowly to his feet. Nick gets up too.*) Go on. Enjoy yourselves, all of you. Leave town, travel, see the world. It's bound to happen. And you know who's going to be sitting here when you get back? I'll tell you who'll be sitting right in that chair. Some Irish fella, some Jewish gentleman is going to be sitting right at this table. Saying the same thing to *his* grandson. And your grandson will be back at the plow! (*Starts out the door, stops, turns.*) And come to think of it, that won't be a bad thing either. Will it, Dora?

DORA. No, sir. (*He exits. Dora starts clearing off. Nick stands in the dining room.*) Well, go on. Hurry. Bring him his checkbook before he falls asleep. (*Nick hurries off R., Dora goes off with plates L. Paul begins to check the table. A Woman, about 40, call her Margery, appears in the hall doorway. She watches Paul.*)

MARGERY. What do you think?

PAUL. (*Working over a chair.*) You're in trouble.

MARGERY. Oh dear. I knew it.

PAUL. It's becoming unglued.

MARGERY. I know the feeling.

PAUL. Coming apart at the seams.

MARGERY. Do you think it's hopeless?

PAUL. Let me check the table. (*He crawls under the table.*)

MARGERY. It shakes very badly. I had a few friends over the other night, and every time we tried to cut our chicken, our water glasses started tinkling frantically. And the chairs creaked and groaned. It was like having dinner at Pompeii.

PAUL. (*Taking out a pocket knife.*) I'm checking the joints here.

MARGERY. It's all very sad. How things run down and fall apart. I used to tell my husband—my *ex*-husband—we have such lovely old things. We should oil them, we should wax them, we should keep them up. But of course I couldn't do everything, and he wouldn't do anything, and now here you are to give us the *coup de grace*.

PAUL. (*Still under table.*) Hey look at this.

MARGERY. What?

PAUL. Look under here.

MARGERY. I don't dare.

PAUL. I'm serious. Look.

MARGERY. Wait till I put on my glasses. (*She puts on her glasses which are hanging from a chain around her neck; then she bends down discreetly.*) Where? I can't see.

PAUL. Under here. Look. This support. See how loose this is?

MARGERY. I can't quite...Wait. (*She gets down on her knees.*)

PAUL. Come on.

MARGERY. All right. (*She crawls under the table.*)

PAUL. See? Look at this support.

MARGERY. I see. It wiggles like mad. (*They are both crawling around under the table now.*)

PAUL. (*Crawling around her.*) And look over there. I'll have to put a whole new piece in over here. See? This is gone.

MARGERY. (*Looking.*) I see.

PAUL. (*Crawling back.*) And... excuse me, please... this pedestal is loose. Probably needs a new dowel. I'll have to ream it out and put in another...

MARGERY. Do you think so?

PAUL. Oh sure. In fact your whole dining room needs to be re-screwed, re-glued, and re-newed. (*His little joke. He comes out from under.*)

MARGERY. Hmmmm. (*She is still under the table.*)

PAUL. What's the matter?

MARGERY. I've never been under a table before.

PAUL. Oh yeah?

MARGERY. It's all just... wood under here, isn't it?

PAUL. That's all it is.

MARGERY. (*Fascinated.*) I mean you'd think a dining room *table* was something special. But it isn't, underneath. It's all just... wood. It's just a couple of big, wide... boards.

PAUL. That's right.

MARGERY. (*Peering.*) What's this, here?

PAUL. What's what?

MARGERY. Well you'll have to come back under here, to see. There's some writing here, burned into the wood.

PAUL. (*Crawling under.*) Where?

MARGERY. Right here. (*She reads, carefully.*) "Freeman's Furniture. Wilkes-Barre, Pa. 1898."

PAUL. (*Under the table.*) Oh that's the manufacturer's mark.

MARGERY. 1898?

PAUL. That's what it says.

MARGERY. But that's not so old.

PAUL. Not if it was made in 1898.

MARGERY. That's not old at all. It's not even an antique. (*Pause.*) It's just... American.

PAUL. There's a lot of these around. They used to crank them out, at the end of the 19th century.

39

MARGERY. Now, aren't I dumb? For years, we've been thinking it's terribly valuable.

PAUL. Well it is, in a sense. It's well made. It's a solid serviceable copy. Based on the English.

MARGERY. Well I'll be darned. You learn something every day. (*They are both sitting side by side, under the table. She looks at him.*) You know a lot about furniture, don't you?

PAUL. I'm beginning to.

MARGERY. Beginning to. I'll bet your father was a cabinet maker or something.

PAUL. My father was a banker.

MARGERY. A *bank*er?

PAUL. And I was a stockbroker. Until I got into this.

MARGERY. I don't believe it.

PAUL. Sure. I decided I wanted to see what I was doing. And touch it. And see the results. So I took up carpentry.

MARGERY. I am amazed. I mean, I *know* some stockbrokers. (*Embarrassed pause. She looks at the strut.*) Is this the support that's bad?

PAUL. That's the one.

MARGERY. What if you put a nail in here?

PAUL. Not a nail. A screw.

MARGERY. (*Crawling over him.*) All right. And another one over here. Or at least some household cement.

PAUL. Well, they have these epoxy glues now...

MARGERY. All right. And maybe cram a matchbook or something in here.

PAUL. Not a matchbook.

MARGERY. A wedge then. A wooden wedge.

PAUL. Good idea.

MARGERY. See? I can do it too. (*In her intensity, she has gotten very close to him physically. They both suddenly realize it, and move away, crawling out from under the table on either side, and brushing themselves off.*) So. Well. Will you be taking the table away? Or can you fix it here?

PAUL. I can fix it here. If you want.

MARGERY. That might make more sense. My husband used to ask for written estimates. Materials and labor.
PAUL. I'll write one up.
MARGERY. Suppose I helped. On the labor.
PAUL. I've never worked that way...
MARGERY. I should learn. I shouldn't be so helpless.
PAUL. O.K. Why not?
MARGERY. Besides, it's not an antique. If I make a mistake, it's not the end of the world, is it?
PAUL. Not at all.
MARGERY. When could we start?
PAUL. Today. Now, if you want.
MARGERY. Then we're a partnership, aren't we? We should have a drink, to celebrate.
PAUL. O.K. (*From off R., we hear voices singing the Thanksgiving hymn:* "*Come Ye Thankful People, Come.*")
MARGERY. What'll we have? Something snappy? Like a martini?
PAUL. No, I gave them up with the stockmarket. How about a beer?
MARGERY. Fine idea. Good, solid beer. If I've *got* it. (*They go off into the kitchen, as Nancy, in her thirties, comes out, carrying a stack of plates and a carving knife and fork. She calls back over her shoulder.*)
NANCY. I've got the plates, Mrs. Driscoll. You've got your hands full with that turkey. (*She sets the plates and carving utensils at the head of the table and calls toward the hall.*) We're ready, everybody! Come on in! (*The singing continues as a Family begins to come into the dining room, to celebrate Thanksgiving dinner. The oldest son Stuart has his Mother on his arm. She is a very vague, very old Old Lady.*)
STUART. ...Now, Mother, I want you to sit next to me, and Fred, you sit on Mother's left, and Ben, you sit opposite her where she can see you, and Nancy and Beth hold up that end of the table, and there we are. (*Genial chatter as everyone sits down. The two Sons push in their Mother's chair. After*

a moment the Old Lady stands up again, looks around distractedly.) What's the matter, Mother?

OLD LADY. I'm not quite sure where I am.

STUART. (*Expansively; arm around her; seating her again.*) You're *here*, Mother. In your own dining room. This is your table, and here are your chairs, and here is the china you got on your trip to England, and here's the silver-handled carving knife which Father used to use.

OLD LADY. Oh yes... (*Genial laughter; adlibbing*: "She's a little tired... It's been a long day..." *The Old Lady gets up again.*) But who are these people? I'm not quite sure who these people are. (*She begins to wander around the room.*)

STUART. (*Following her around.*) It's me, Mother: Stuart. Your son. And here's Fred, and Ben, and Nancy, and Beth. We're all here, Mother.

NANCY. (*Going into the kitchen.*) I'll get the turkey. That might help her focus.

STUART. Yes. (*To Old Lady.*) Mrs. Driscoll is here, Mother. Right in the kitchen, where she's always been. And your grandchildren. All your grandchildren were here. Don't you remember? They ate first, at the children's table, and now they're out in back playing touch football. You watched them, Mother. (*He indicates the French doors.*)

OLD LADY. Oh yes... (*She sits down again at the other end of the table. Nancy comes out from the kitchen, carrying a large platter. Appropriate Oh's and Ah's from Group.*)

STUART. And look, Mother. Here's Nancy with the turkey.... Put it right over there, Nancy...See, Mother? Isn't it a beautiful bird? And I'm going to carve it just the way Father did, and give you a small piece of the breast and a dab of dressing, just as always, Mother. (*He sharpens the carving knive officiously.*)

OLD LADY. (*Still staring out into the garden.*) Just as always...

STUART. (*As he sharpens.*) And Fred will have the drumstick— am I right, Fred?—and Beth gets the wishbone, and Ben ends up with the Pope's nose, am I right, Ben? (*Genial in-group laughter.*)

42

NANCY. Save some for Mrs. Driscoll.

STUART. I always do, Nancy. Mrs. Driscoll likes the second joint.

OLD LADY. This is all very nice, but I think I'd like to go home.

STUART. (*Patiently, as he carves.*) You are home, Mother. You've lived here fifty-two years.

BEN. Fifty-four.

BETH. Forever.

STUART. Ben, pass this plate down to Mother . . .

OLD LADY. (*Getting up.*) Thank you very much, but I really do think it's time to go.

NANCY. Uh-oh.

STUART. (*Going to her.*) Mother . . .

BETH. Oh dear.

OLD LADY. Will someone drive me home, please? I live at eighteen Summer Street with my mother and sisters.

BETH. What will we do?

STUART. (*Going to Old Lady.*) It's not there now, Mother. Don't you remember? We drove down. There's a big building there now.

OLD LADY. (*Holding out her hand.*) Thank you very much for asking me . . . Thank you for having me to your house. (*She begins to go around the table, thanking people.*)

FRED. Mother! I'm Fred! Your son!

OLD LADY. Isn't that nice? Thank you. I've had a perfectly lovely time . . . Thank you . . . Thank you so much. (*She shakes hands with Nancy.*) It's been absolutely lovely . . . Thank you, thank you.

STUART. Quickly. Let's sing to her.

BETH. Sing?

STUART. She likes singing. We used to sing to her whenever she'd get upset . . . Fred, Ben. Quickly. Over here.

OLD LADY. (*Wandering distracted around.*) Now I can't find my gloves. Where would my gloves be? I can't go out without my gloves.

BEN. What song? I can't remember any of the songs.

STUART. Sure you can. Come on. Hmmmmm. (*He sounds a note. The others try to find their parts.*)

BEN & FRED. Hmmmmmmmm.

OLD LADY. I need my gloves, I need my hat...

STUART. (*Singing.*)
"As the blackbird in the spring...

OTHERS. (*Joining in.*)
'Neath the willow tree...
Sat and piped, I heard him sing,
Sing of Aura Lee...

(*They sing in pleasant, amateurish, corny harmony. The Old Lady stops fussing, turns her head, and listens. The other women remain at the table.*)

MEN. (*Singing.*)
Aura Lee, Aura Lee, Maid of Golden Hair...
Sunshine came along with thee, and swallows in the air."

OLD LADY. I love music. Every person in our family could play a different instrument. (*She sits in a chair along the wall, Down Right.*)

STUART. (*To his brothers.*) She's coming around. Quickly. Second verse.

MEN. (*Singing with more confidence now; more daring harmony.*)
"In thy blush the rose was born,
Music, when you spake,
Through thine azure eye the morn
Sparkling seemed to break.
Aura Lee, Aura Lee, Maid of Golden Hair,
Sunshine came along with thee, and swallows in the air."

(*They hold a long note at the end. The Old Lady claps. Everyone claps.*)

OLD LADY. That was absolutely lovely.

STUART. Thank you, Mother.

OLD LADY. But now I've simply got to go home. Would you call my carriage, please? And someone find my hat and gloves. It's very late, and my mother gets very nervous if I'm not home in time for tea. (*She heads for the hall.*)

STUART. (*To no one in particular.*) Look, Fred, Ben, we'll drive her down, and show her everything. The new office complex where her house was. The entrance to the Thruway. The new Howard Johnson's motel. Everything! And she'll see that nothing's there at all.

FRED. I'll bring the car around.

STUART. I'll get her coat.

BEN. I'm coming, too.

STUART. We'll just have to go through the motions. (*The brothers hurry after their mother. Nancy and Beth are left alone onstage. Pause. Then they begin to stack the dishes.*)

NANCY. That's scary.

BETH. I know it.

NANCY. I suddenly feel so... precarious.

BETH It could happen to us all.

NANCY. No, but it's as if we didn't exist. As if we were all just... ghosts, or something. Even her own sons. She walked right by them.

BETH. And guess who walked right by *us*.

NANCY. (*Glancing off.*) Yes... (*Pause.*) Know what I'd like?

BETH. What?

NANCY. A good stiff drink.

BETH. I'm with you.

NANCY. I'll bet Mrs. Driscoll could use a drink, too.

BETH. Bet she could.

NANCY. (*Deciding.*) Let's go out and ask her!

BETH. Mrs. Driscoll?

NANCY. Let's! (*Pause.*)

BETH. All right.

NANCY. Let's go and have a drink with Mrs. Driscoll, and then dig into this turkey, and help her with the dishes, and then figure out how to get through the rest of the goddamn day! (*They go off, into the kitchen. The table is clear, the dining room is empty.*)

END OF ACT I

ACT II

The dining room is empty. The light suggests that it is about three in the afternoon.

After a moment, a Girl's voice is heard Off Right, from the front hall.

GIRL'S VOICE. Mom? MOM? Anybody home? (*Silence; then more softly.*) See? I told you. She isn't here. (*Sarah appears in the doorway, with Helen behind her.*)
HELEN. Where is she?
SARAH. She works. At a boutique. Four days a week. And my father's away on business. In Atlanta. Or Denver or somewhere. Anyway. Come on. I'll show you where they keep the liquor.
HELEN. My mom's always there when I get home from school. Always.
SARAH. Bummer.
HELEN. And if she isn't, my grandmother comes in.
SARAH. The liquor's in the pantry. (*Sarah goes out through kitchen door, L. Helen stays in the dining room.*)
HELEN. (*Taking in the dining room.*) Oh. Hey. Neat-o.
SARAH'S VOICE. (*From within.*) What?
HELEN. This *room.*
SARAH'S VOICE. (*Over clinking of liquor bottles.*) That's our dining room.
HELEN. I know. But it's viciously nice.
SARAH. (*Coming out of kitchen, carrying two bottles.*) Which do you want? Gin or vodka?
HELEN. (*Wandering around the room.*) You decide.

46

SARAH (*Looking at bottles.*) Well there's more gin, so it's less chance they'll notice.

HELEN. Gin, then.

SARAH. But the reason there's more gin is that I put water in it last week.

HELEN. Vodka, then.

SARAH. Tell you what. We'll mix in a little of both. (*She goes into the kitchen.*)

HELEN. O.K.... Do you *use* this room.

SARAH. Oh sure.

HELEN. Special occasions, huh? When the relatives come to visit?

SARAH'S VOICE. Every night.

HELEN. Every NIGHT?

SARAH'S VOICE. Well at least every night they're both home.

HELEN. Really?

SARAH (*Coming in, carrying two glasses.*) Oh sure. Whenever they're home, my father insists that we all eat in the dining room at seven o'clock. (*Hands Helen her drink.*) Here. Gin and vodka and Fresca. The boys are bringing the pot.

HELEN. (*Drinking.*) Mmmm...It must be nice, eating here.

SARAH. (*Slouching in a chair.*) Oh yeah sure you bet. We have to lug things out, and lug things back, and nobody can begin till everything's cold, and we're supposed to carry on a decent conversation, and everyone has to finish before anyone can get up, and it sucks, if you want to know. It sucks out loud. (*They drink.*)

HELEN. We eat in the kitchen.

SARAH. Can you watch TV while you eat?

HELEN. We used to. We used to watch the local news and weather.

SARAH. That's something At least you don't have to talk.

HELEN. But now we can't watch it. My mother read in *Family Circle* that TV was bad at meals. So now we turn on the stereo and listen to semi-classical music.

SARAH. My parents said they tried eating in the kitchen when I went to boarding school. But when I got kicked out, they

47

moved back in here. It's supposed to give me some sense of stability.

HELEN. Do you think it does?

SARAH. Shit no! It just makes me nervous. They take the telephone off the hook, so no one can call, and my brother gets itchy about his homework, and when my sister had anorexia, she still had to sit here and *watch*, for God's sake, and my parents spend most of the meal bitching, and the whole thing bites, Helen. It really bites. It bites the big one. Want another?

HELEN No thanks.

SARAH. I do ... You call the boys and tell them it's all clear. (*Sarah goes back into the kitchen.*)

HELEN. (*Calling toward kitchen.*) Sarah ...

SARAH'S VOICE. (*Within.*) What?

HELEN. When the boys come over, can we have our drinks in here? (*Kate, a woman in her mid-forties, comes out. She carries a small tray containing a teapot, two teacups, sugar and creamer. She sits at the table and watches the teapot.*)

SARAH'S VOICE. (*Within.*) In the *dining* room?

HELEN. I mean, wouldn't it be cool, sitting around this shiny table with Eddie and Duane, drinking gin and Fresca and vodka?

SARAH. (*Coming out from the kitchen.*) No way. Absolutely no way. In here? I'd get all up tight in here. (*She heads for the hall.*) Now come on. Let's *call* them. (*Helen starts after her.*) Having *boys* in the *di*ning room? Jesus, Helen. You really are a wimp sometimes. (*They go out, R., Helen looking back over her shoulder at the dining room.*)

KATE. (*Calling toward hallway.*) I'm in here, Gordon. I made tea. (*Gordon comes in from the hall. He is about her age. He is buttoning his shirt, carrying his jacket and tie slung over his shoulder.*)

GORDON. Tea?

KATE. Tea.

GORDON. Why tea?

KATE. Because I like it. I love it. (*Pause.*) Or would you like a drink?

48

GORDON. No thanks.

KATE. Go ahead. Don't worry about me. I'm all over that. We even have it in the house, and I never touch it.

GORDON. No thanks, Kate.

KATE. Then have tea. It's very good. It's Earl Gray.

GORDON. I ought to be getting back.

KATE. Gordon, please. Have tea. (*Pause.*)

GORDON. All right.

KATE. Thank you. (*She begins to pour him a cup.*)

GORDON. (*Ironically.*) Tea in the dining room.

KATE. Where else? Should we huddle guiltily over the kitchen table?

GORDON. No.

KATE. Then tea in the dining room...What would you like? Lemon or milk?

GORDON. Whatever.

KATE. Gordon.

GORDON. Milk, then. No sugar.

KATE. Milk it is. (*She hands him a cup.*) Well sit down, for heaven's sake.

GORDON. (*Not sitting.*) I thought I heard a sound.

KATE. Oh really? And what sound did you hear? A distant lawn-mower? A faulty burglar alarm?

GORDON. I thought I heard a car.

KATE. What? A car? On this god-forsaken street? Should we rush to the window? Cheer? Wave flags?

GORDON. Go easy, Kate.

KATE. Well I doubt very much that you heard a car.

GORDON. (*Listening.*) It stopped.

KATE. The sound?

GORDON. The *car*. The car stopped.

KATE. All right, Gordon. You heard a car stop. But it's not Ed's car, is it? Because Ed, as you and I well know, is in Amsterdam, or Rotterdam, or who-gives-a-damn until next Tuesday. (*Reaching for his hand.*) Now sit *down*. Please. Let's have tea, for heaven's sake. (*He sits on the edge of his chair.*) Now when can we meet again?

GORDON. (*Jumping up.*) I heard a car door slam.

KATE. Oh really. That's because cars have doors. And people when they get really frustrated feel like slamming them.

GORDON. I'm going.

KATE. I see how it is—a quick tumble with the bored wife of your best friend.

GORDON. Someone's at the front door.

KATE. No...

GORDON. Yes. Someone with a key! (*Kate jumps up, They listen.*)

KATE. (*Whispering.*) Now you've got to stay. (*Gordon quickly puts on his coat. A boy's voice is heard calling from the hall.*)

BOY'S VOICE. Mom!

KATE. Lord help us.

BOY'S VOICE. I'm home, Mom!

KATE. (*Grimly to Gordon.*) Now you've got to have tea.

BOY'S VOICE. Mom?

KATE. (*Calling out.*) We're in the dining room, dear. (*Chris slides into view from R. He is about seventeen, carries a duffle-bag. Kate goes to him effusively.*) Darling! How'd you get here?

CHRIS. I took a cab from the bus station. (*Kate embraces him. He looks at Gordon.*)

KATE. You look marvelous! Taller than ever! Say hello to Uncle Gordon.

GORDON. Hi, Chris. Welcome home.

CHRIS. (*Coolly.*) Hi.

KATE. What's this? Is this what they teach you at Deerfield? Not to shake hands? Not to call people by name?

CHRIS. Hello, Uncle Gordon. (*They shake hands.*)

GORDON. Hi, Chris.

KATE. But what brings you home, my love? I expected you Saturday.

CHRIS. I got honors.

KATE. Honors?

CHRIS. You get two days early if you get an over-85 average.

KATE. But then you should have telephoned.

CHRIS. I wanted to surprise you. (*Pause.*)

50

GORDON. I ought to go.

KATE. Nonsense. Have more tea. Chris, would you like tea? I was taking a nap, and Gordon stopped by, and we thought we'd have tea. Have some tea, dear. Or a Coke. Have a Coke. Or shall I get you a beer? How about a beer for a big boy who gets honors?

CHRIS. No, thanks.

GORDON. I'd really better go.

KATE. You won't have more tea.

GORDON. Can't. Sorry.

KATE. All right, then. Goodbye.

GORDON. (*Shaking hands with her stiffly.*) Goodbye...Goodbye, Chris. (*He tries to shake hands with Chris.*)

CHRIS. (*Turning away.*) Goodbye. (*Gordon goes, quickly, R. Kate starts to put the tea things back on the tray.*)

KATE. He wanted to talk to me about stocks. I inherited some stock he thinks I should sell, and so he stopped by—

CHRIS. Where's Dad?

KATE. He's in Europe, darling. As I think I wrote you. He'll be home Tuesday. (*She starts for the kitchen with the tray.*)

CHRIS. Oh Mom.

KATE. (*Stopping, turning.*) And what does that mean, pray tell? "Oh Mom." (*He turns away.*) I'd like to know, please, what that means? (*He shakes his head.*) I happened to be having *tea*, Christopher. It happens to be a very old custom. Your grandmother used to have tea at this very table with this same china every afternoon. All sorts of people would stop by. All the time. I'd come home from school, and there she'd be. Serving tea. It's a delightful old custom, sweetheart. - (*He starts for the hall.*) Where are you going? I asked you a question, please. We don't just walk away. (*Chris walks out of the room. Kate calls after Chris.*) Chris, I am talking to you. I am talking to you, and I am your mother, and the least you can do is... (*She follows him out into the hall, still carrying the tray. A Young Man named Tony comes in from the kitchen, decked out with a camera and various pieces of photographic equipment. He begins to test the room with his light meter. He finds an area by a chair which pleases him. He calls toward the kitchen.)*

TONY. Would you mind setting up over here, Aunt Harriet? I want to get you in the late afternoon light. *(Aunt Harriet, a woman of about sixty, appears at the kitchen door, carrying another tray, glittering with old china and crystal.)*

AUNT HARRIET. *(Beaming proudly.)* Certainly, Tony. *(She goes to where he indicates, puts down her tray, and begins to set a place at the table.)* Now I thought I'd use this Irish linen place mat with matching napkin, that my husband—who was what? Your great uncle—inherited from his sister. They have to be washed and ironed by hand every time they're used. *(She places the place mat; he photographs it.)* And then of course the silver, which was given to us as a wedding present by your great-grandmother. You see? Three prong forks. Pistol-handled knives. Spoon with rat tail back. All Williamsburg pattern. This should be polished at least every two weeks. *(She sets a place as he photographs each item. She becomes more and more at home with the camera.)* And then this is Stafford-shire, as is the butter plate. All of this is Bone. The wine glasses are early Steuben, but the goblets and finger bowls are both Waterford. None of this goes in the dishwasher, of course. It's all far too delicate for detergents. *(The place is all set. She surveys it proudly.)*

TONY. Finger bowls?

AUNT HARRIET. Oh yes. Our side of the family always used finger bowls between the salad and the dessert.

TONY. Would you show me how they worked?

AUNT HARRIET. Certainly, dear. *(He continues to snap pictures of her as she talks.)* You see the maid would take away the salad plate—like this—*(She puts a plate aside to her right.)* And then she'd put down the finger bowls in front of us. Like this. *(She does.)* They would be filled approximately halfway with cool water. And there might be a little rose floating in it. Or a sliver of lemon…Now of course, we'd have our napkins in our laps—like this. *(She sits down, shakes out her napkin, puts it discreetly in her lap.)* And then we'd dip our fingers

52

into the finger bowl...gently, gently...and then we'd wiggle them and shake them out...and then dab them on our napkins ...and then dab our lips...then, of course, the maids would take them away... (*She moves the finger bowl aside.*) And in would come a nice sherbert or chocolate mousse! (*She beams at the camera, at last used to it. He snaps her picture.*)

TONY. Thanks, Aunt Harriet. That was terrific. (*He begins to pack up his photographic gear.*)

AUNT HARRIET. You're welcome. Now, Tony, dear, tell me again what all this is for. I didn't quite understand over the telephone.

TONY. This is a classroom project. For Amherst.

AUNT HARRIET. Oh, my. A project. (*She stands up.*) In what, pray tell.

TONY. Anthropology, actually.

AUNT HARRIET. And*thropology*. Heavens! (*She starts to return items to her tray.*) What does that have to do with this?

TONY. Well you see we're studying the eating habits of various vanishing cultures. For example, someone is talking about the Kikuyus of Northern Kenya. And my roommate is doing the Cree Indians of Saskatchewan. And my professor suggested I do a slide show on us.

AUNT HARRIET. Us?

TONY. The Wasps. Of Northeastern United States. (*Pause.*)

AUNT HARRIET. I see.

TONY. You can learn a lot about a culture from how it eats.

AUNT HARRIET. (*With increasing coldness.*) Such as what?

TONY. Well. Consider the finger bowls, for example. There you have an almost neurotic obsession with cleanliness, relflecting the guilt which comes with the last stages of capitalism. Or notice the unnecessary accumulation of glass and china, and the compulsion to display it. Or the subtle hint of aggression in those pistol-handled knives.

AUNT HARRIET. I think I'll ask you to leave, Tony.

TONY. Aunt Harriet...

AUNT HARRIET. I was going to invite you to stay for a cocktail, but now I won't.

53

TONY. Please, Aunt Harriet... (*He begins to gather up his equipment.*)

AUNT HARRIET. Out! Right now! Before I telephone long distance to your mother! (*Tony backs toward the hallway.*) Vanishing culture, my eye! I forbid you to mention my name in the classroom! Or show one glimpse of my personal property! And you can tell that professor of yours, I've got a good mind to drive up to Amherst, with this pistol-handled butter knife on the seat beside me, and cut off his anthropological balls! (*Tony runs hurriedly from the room. Harriet returns to her tray proudly, and carries it back into the kitchen, As She goes, An Older Man, called Jim, comes in from the hall, followed by his daughter, Meg. He is in his late sixties, she is about thirty.*)

MEG. Where are you going now, Daddy?

JIM. I think your mother might want a drink.

MEG. She's reading to the children.

JIM. That's why she might want one.

MEG. She wants no such thing, Dad.

JIM. Then I want one.

MEG. Now? It's not even five.

JIM. Well then let's go see how the Red Sox are doing. (*He starts back out, R.*)

MEG. Daddy, *stop!*

JIM. Stop what?

MEG. Avoiding me. Ever since I arrived, we haven't been able to talk.

JIM. Good Lord, what do you mean? Seems to me everybody's been talking continuously and simultaneously from the moment you got off the plane.

MEG. Alone, Daddy. I mean *alone*. And you *know* I mean alone.

JIM. All right. We'll talk. (*Sits down.*) Right here in the dining room. Good place to talk. Why not? Matter of fact, I'm kind of tired. It's been a long day.

MEG. I love this room. I've always loved it. Always.

JIM. Your mother and I still use it. Now and then. Once a week. Mrs. Robinson still comes in and cooks us a nice dinner and we have it in here. Still. Lamb chops. Broilers—

MEG. (*Suddenly.*) I've left him, Daddy.

JIM. Oh well now, a little vacation . . .

MEG. I've left him permanently.

JIM. Yes, well, permanently is a very long word . . .

MEG. I can't live with him, Dad. We don't get along at all.

JIM. Oh well, you may think that now . . .

MEG. Could we live here, Dad?

JIM. Here?

MEG. For a few months.

JIM. With three small children?

MEG. While I work out my life. (*Pause. Jim takes out a pocket watch and looks at it.*)

JIM. What time is it? A little after five. I think the sun is over the yardarm, don't you? Or if it isn't, it should be. I think it's almost permissible for you and me to have a little drink, Meg.

MEG. Can we stay here, Dad?

JIM. Make us a drink, Meggie.

MEG. All right. (*She goes into the kitchen; the door, of course, remains open.*)

JIM. (*Calling to her.*) I'd like Scotch, sweetheart. Make it reasonably strong. You'll find the silver measuring gizmo in the drawer by the trays. I want two shots and a splash of water. And I like to use that big glass with the pheasant on it. And not too much ice. (*He gets up and moves around the table.*)

MEG'S VOICE. (*Within.*) All right.

JIM. I saw Mimi Mott the other day . . . Can you hear me?

MEG'S VOICE. (*Within.*) I can hear you, Dad.

JIM. There she was, being a very good sport with her third husband. Her third. Who's deaf as a post and extremely disagreeable. So I took her aside—can you hear me?

MEG'S VOICE. (*Within.*) I'm listening, Dad.

JIM. I took her aside, and I said, "Now Mimi, tell me the truth. If you had made half as much effort with your first husband as you've made with the last two, don't you think you'd still be married to him?" I asked her that. Point blank. And you know what Mimi said? She said, "Maybe." That's exactly what she said. "Maybe." If she had made the effort. (*Meg returns with two glasses. She gives one to Jim.*)

MEG. That's your generation, Dad.

JIM. That's every generation.

MEG. It's not mine.

JIM. Every generation has to make an effort.

MEG. I won't go back to him, Dad. I want to be here.

JIM. (*Looking at his glass.*) I wanted the glass with the pheasant on it.

MEG. I think the kids used it.

JIM. Oh. (*Pause. He drinks, moves away from her.*)

MEG. So can we stay, Dad?

JIM. I sleep in your room now. Your mother kicked me out because I snore. And we use the boys' room now to watch TV.

MEG. I'll use the guest room.

JIM. And the children?

MEG. They can sleep on the third floor. In the maid's rooms.

JIM. We closed them off. Because of the oil bills.

MEG. I don't care, Dad. We'll work it out. Please. (*Pause. He sits down at the other end of the table.*)

JIM. Give it another try first.

MEG. No.

JIM. Another try.

MEG. He's got someone else now, Dad. She's living there right now. She's moved in.

JIM. Then fly back and kick her out.

MEG. Oh, Dad . . .

JIM. I'm serious. You don't know this, but that's what your mother did. One time I became romantically involved with Mrs. Shoemaker. We took a little trip together. To Sea Island. Your mother got wind of it, and came right down, and told Betty Shoemaker to get on the next train. That's all there was to it. Now why don't you do that? Go tell this woman to peddle her papers elsewhere. We'll sit with the children while you do.

MEG. I've got someone too, Dad. (*Pause.*)

JIM. You mean you've had a little fling.

MEG. I've been going with someone.

JIM. A little fling.

MEG. I've been living with him.

JIM. Where was your husband?

MEG. He stayed with his girl.

JIM. And your children?

MEG. Oh they ... came and went.

JIM. It sounds a little ... complicated.

MEG. It is, Dad. That's why I needed to come home. (*Pause. He drinks.*)

JIM. Now let's review the bidding, may we? Do you plan to marry this new man?

MEG. No.

JIM. You're not in love with him?

MEG. No. He's already married, anyway.

JIM. And he's decided he loves his wife.

MEG. No.

JIM. But you've decided you don't love him.

MEG. Yes.

JIM. Or your husband.

MEG. Yes.

JIM. And your husband's fallen in love with someone else.

MEG. He lives with someone else.

JIM. And your children ... my grandchildren ... come and go among these various households.

MEG. Yes. Sort of. Yes.

JIM. Sounds extremely complicated.

MEG. It is, Dad. It really is. (*Pause. He drinks, thinks, gets up, paces.*)

JIM. Well then it seems to me the first thing you do is simplify things. That's the first thing. You ask the man you're living with to leave, you sue your husband for divorce, you hold onto your house, you keep the children in their present schools, you—

MEG. There's someone else, Dad. *(Pause.)*

JIM. Someone else?

MEG. Someone else entirely.

JIM. A third person.

MEG. Yes.

JIM. What was that movie your mother and I liked so much? *The Third Man? (He sits, D.L.)*

MEG. It's not a man, Dad. *(Pause.)*

JIM. Not a man.

MEG. It's a woman.

JIM. A woman.

MEG. I've been involved with a woman, Dad, but it's not working, and I don't know who I am, and I've got to touch *base*, Daddy. I want to be here. *(She kneels at his feet. Pause. Jim gets slowly to his feet. He points to his glass.)*

JIM. I think I'll get a repair. Would you like a repair? I'll take your glass. I'll get us both repairs. *(He takes her glass and goes out to the kitchen, leaving the door open.)*

MEG. *(Moving around the dining room.)* I'm all mixed up, Dad. I'm all over the ball park. I've been seeing a Crisis Counselor, and I've taken a part-time job, and I've been jogging two miles a day, and none of it's working, Dad. I want to come home. I want to take my children to the Zoo, and the Park Lake, and the Art Gallery, and do all those things you and Mother used to do with all of us. I want to start again, Dad. I want to start all over again. *(Jim comes out from the kitchen, now carrying three glasses.)*

JIM. I made one for your mother. And I found the glass with the pheasant on it. In the trash. Somebody broke it. *(He crosses for the doorway, R.)* So let's have a nice cocktail with your mother, and see if we can get the children to sit quietly while we do.

MEG. You don't want us here, do you, Dad?

JIM. *(Stopping.)* Of course we do, darling. A week, ten days. You're most welcome.

MEG. *(Desperately.)* I can't go back, Dad!

58

JIM. (*Quietly.*) Neither can I, sweetheart. Neither can I. (*He shuffles on out. Meg stands for a moment in the dining room, then hurries out after him as Emily, a woman of about thirty-five comes in and looks at the table.*)

EMILY. (*Distractedly.*) I don't know whether to eat, or not. (*Her son David comes in. He's about fourteen.*)

DAVID. What's the trouble, Mother?

EMILY. I don't know whether to eat or not. Your father and I were sitting in the living room, having a perfectly pleasant cocktail together, when all of a sudden that stupid telephone rang, and now he's holed up in the bedroom, talking away. (*She closes the kitchen door.*)

DAVID. Who's he talking to?

EMILY. I don't know. I don't even know. I think it's someone from the club. (*Claire, her daughter, comes on. She's about sixteen.*)

CLAIRE. Are we eating or not?

EMILY. I simply don't know. (*Bertha, the Maid, sticks her head out of the kitchen door.*) I don't know whether to go ahead or not, Bertha. Mr. Thatcher is still on the telephone.

CLAIRE. Couldn't we at least start the soup?

EMILY. I don't know. I just don't know. Oh, let's wait five more minutes, Bertha.

BERTHA. Yes, Mrs. (*Bertha disappears. Emily, David, and Claire sit down.*)

EMILY. Honestly, that telephone! I could wring its neck! It should be banned, it should be outlawed, between six and eight in the evening. (*The Father comes in hurriedly from the hall. His name is Standish.*)

STANDISH. I've got to go.

EMILY. (*Standing up.*) Go? Go where?

STANDISH. Out. (*Bertha comes in with the soup tureen.*)

EMILY. You mean you can't even sit down and have some of Bertha's nice celery soup?

STANDISH. I can't even finish my cocktail. Something very bad has happened.

EMILY. Bertha, would you mind very much putting the soup back in a saucepan and keeping it on a low flame. We'll call you when we're ready.

BERTHA. Yes, Mrs. (*Bertha goes out, Standish takes Emily aside, D.L.*)

EMILY. (*Hushed tones.*) Now what on earth is the matter?

STANDISH. Henry was insulted down at the club.

EMILY. Insulted?

CLAIRE. (*From the table.*) Uncle Henry?

STANDISH. (*Ignoring Claire; to Emily.*) Binky Byers made a remark to him in the steam bath.

EMILY. Oh no!

DAVID. What did he say, Dad?

CLAIRE. Yes, what did he say?

STANDISH. I believe I was speaking to your mother. (*Pause. The children are quelled.*) Binky made a remark, and apparently a number of the newer members laughed. Poor Henry was so upset he had to put on his clothes and leave. He called me from Mother's.

EMILY. Oh no, oh no.

STANDISH. I telephoned the club. I spoke to several people who had been in the steam bath. They confirmed the incident. I asked to speak to Binky Byers. He refused to come to the phone. And so I've got to do something about it.

EMILY. Oh dear, oh dear.

DAVID. Won't you tell us what he said to Uncle Henry, Dad?

STANDISH. I will not. I will not dignify the remark by repeating it.

DAVID. Oh come on, Dad. We're not babies.

EMILY. Yes, Standish. Really.

STANDISH. He said—(*Checks himself.*) Claire, I want you to leave the room.

CLAIRE. Why? I'm older.

EMILY. Yes. She should know. Everybody should know. These are different times. (*Bertha comes out.*) We're not quite ready yet, Bertha. (*Bertha goes right back in.*)

60

EMILY. Now go on, Standish. Be frank. This is a family.

STANDISH. (*Hesitatingly; looking from one to the other.*) Mr. Byers...made an unfortunate remark...having to do with your Uncle Henry's...private life. (*Pause. The children don't get it.*)

EMILY. I'm afraid you'll have to be more specific, dear.

STANDISH. (*Taking a deep breath.*) Mr. Byers, who had obviously been drinking since early afternoon, approached your Uncle Henry in the steam bath, and alluded in very specific terms to his personal relationships.

CLAIRE. What personal relationships?

STANDISH. His—associations. In the outside world. (*Pause.*)

DAVID. I don't get it.

EMILY. Darling, Mr. Byers must have made some unnecessary remarks about your Uncle Henry's bachelor attachments.

DAVID. You mean Uncle Harry is a *fruit*?

STANDISH. (*Wheeling on him.*) I WON'T HAVE THAT WORD IN THIS HOUSE!

DAVID. I was just...

EMILY. He got it from school, dear.

STANDISH. I don't care if he got it from God! I will not have it in this house! The point is my own *brother* was wounded at his *club*! (*Pause.*)

EMILY. But what can you do, dear?

STANDISH. Go down there.

EMILY. To your mother's?

STANDISH. To the *club*! I'll demand a public apology from Binky in front of the entire grille.

EMILY. But if he won't even come to the telephone...

STANDISH. I'll have to fight him.

EMILY. Oh, Standish.

STANDISH. I have to.

CLAIRE. Oh, Daddy...

STANDISH. I can't let the remark stand.

DAVID. Can I come with you, Dad?

STANDISH. You may not. I want you home with your mother.

61

(He starts for the door.)

EMILY. Standish, for heaven's sake!

STANDISH. No arguments, please.

EMILY. But Binky Byers is half your age! And twice your size!

STANDISH. It makes no difference.

EMILY. I think he was on the boxing team at Dartmouth!

STANDISH. No difference whatsoever.

EMILY. What about your bad shoulder? What about your hernia?

STANDISH. I'm sorry, I imagine I shall be seriously hurt. But I can't stand idly by.

CLAIRE. *(Tearfully.)* Oh, Daddy, please don't go. *(Bertha comes out of the kitchen.)*

BERTHA. The lamb will be overdone, Mrs.

EMILY. And it's a beautiful *lamb*, Standish!

STANDISH. *(Shouting them down.)* Now *listen* to me! *All* of you! *(Bertha has been heading back to the kitchen.)* And you, too, Bertha! *(He points toward a chair D.L. Bertha crosses, as everyone watches her. She sits on the edge of the chair. Everyone turns back to Standish.)* There is nothing, nothing I'd rather do in this world, than sit down at this table with all of you and have some of Bertha's fine celery soup, followed by a leg of lamb with mint sauce and roast potatoes. Am I right about the sauce and the potatoes, Bertha?

BERTHA. Yes, sir.

STANDISH. There is nothing I'd rather do than that. But I have to forego it. My own brother has been publicly insulted at his club. And that means our family has been insulted. And when the family has been insulted, that means this table, these chairs, this room, and all of us in it, including you, Bertha, are being treated with scorn. And so if I stayed here, if I sat down with all of you now, I wouldn't be able to converse, I wouldn't be able to laugh, I wouldn't be able to correct your grammar, David, I wouldn't be able to enjoy your fine meal,

Bertha. (*Turning to Emily.*) I wouldn't even be able to kiss my handsome wife goodbye. (*He kisses her. It's a passionate kiss.*) Goodbye, dear.

EMILY. Goodbye, darling. (*He kisses Claire.*)

STANDISH. Goodbye, Winkins.

CLAIRE. Goodbye, Daddy. (*He shakes hands with David.*)

STANDISH. Goodbye, David.

DAVID. So long, Dad. Good luck.

STANDISH. Goodbye, Bertha.

BERTHA. Goodbye, sir. God bless you.

STANDISH. Thank you very much indeed. (*He goes out. Pause.*)

EMILY. (*Now all business.*) Of course we can't eat now, Bertha. Have something yourself, and let people raid the ice-box later on.

BERTHA. Yes, Mrs.

EMILY. And the children can have lamb hash on Saturday.

BERTHA. Yes, Mrs. (*Bertha goes off.*)

EMILY. David: you and I will drive down to the club, and wait for the outcome in the visitor's lounge.

DAVID. O.K., Mother.

EMILY. So get a book. Get a good book. Get *Ivanhoe*. We could be quite a while.

DAVID. O.K. (*He goes out.*)

EMILY. And Claire: I want you to stay here, and hold the fort.

CLAIRE. All right, Mother.

EMILY. Get on the telephone to Doctor Russell. I don't care whether he's having dinner or in the operating room. Tell him to be at the club to give your father first aid.

CLAIRE. All right, Mother.

EMILY. And then study your French.

CLAIRE. All right. (*She starts out, then stops.*) Mother?

EMILY. (*Impatiently in the doorway.*) What, for heaven's sake?

CLAIRE. Is it true about Uncle Henry?

EMILY. Well it may be, sweetheart. But you don't say it to *him*. And you don't say it at the *club*. And you don't say it within a ten-mile radius of your *father*. Now goodbye. (*Emily rushes off, R, followed by Claire. An Old Man and his middle-aged son come on from R. The Old Man is Harvey, his son is Dick. The light is dim in the dining room now, except D.C., by the "French windows".*)

HARVEY. (*As he enters.*) We'll talk in here. No one will disturb us. Nobody comes near a dining room any more. The thought of sitting down with a number of intelligent, attractive people to enjoy good food well cooked and properly served... that apparently doesn't occur to people any more. Nowadays people eat in kitchens, or in living rooms, standing around, balancing their plates like jugglers. Soon they'll be eating in bathrooms. Well why not? Simplify the process considerably.

DICK. Sit down somewhere, Pop.

HARVEY. (*Coming well D., pulling a chair down, away from the table.*) I'll sit here. We can look out. There's a purple finch who comes to the feeder every evening. Brings his young. (*Dick pulls up a chair beside him. Behind, in the dim light, three Women begin to set the table, this time for an elaborate dinner A great white table cloth, candles, flowers, the works. The process should be reverential, quiet, and muted, not to distract from the scene D. Taking an envelope from his inside pocket.*) Now. I want to go over my funeral with you.

DICK. Pop—

HARVEY. I want to do it. There are only a few more apples left in the barrel for me.

DICK. You've been saying that for years, Pop.

HARVEY. Well this time it's true. So I want to go over this, please. You're my eldest son. I can't do it with anyone else. Your mother starts to cry, your brother isn't here, and your sister gets distracted. So concentrate, please, on my funeral.

DICK. All right, Pop.

HARVEY. (*Taking out a typewritten document.*) First, here is my obituary. For both newspapers. I dictated it to Miss Kovak

64

down at the office, and I've read it over twice, and it's what I want. It's thorough without being self-congratulatory. I mention my business career, my civic commitments, and of course my family. I even touch on my recreational life. I give my lowest score in golf and the weight of the sailfish I caught off the Keys. The papers will want to cut both items, but don't you let them.

DICK. O.K., Pop.

HARVEY. I also want them to print this picture. (*He shows it.*) It was taken when I was elected to chair the Symphony drive. I think it will do. I don't look too young to die, nor so old it won't make any difference.

DICK. All right, Pop.

HARVEY. (*Fussing with other documents.*) Now I want the funeral service announced at the end of the obituary, and to occur three days later. That will give people time to postpone their trips and adjust their appointments. And I want it at three-thirty in the afternoon. This gives people time to digest their lunch and doesn't obligate us to feed them dinner. Notice I've underlined the word *church*. Mr. Fayerweather might try to squeeze the service into the chapel, but don't let him. I've lived in this city all my life, and know a great many people, and I want everyone to have a seat and feel comfortable. If you see people milling around the door, go right up to them and find them a place, even if you have to use folding chairs. Are we clear on that?

DICK. Yes, Pop. (*By now the table has been mostly set behind them. The Women have gone.*)

HARVEY. I've listed the following works to be played by Mrs. Manchester at the organ. This Bach, this Handel, this Schubert. All lively, you'll notice. Nothing gloomy, nothing grim. I want the service to start promptly with a good rousing hymn—*Onward Christian Soldiers*—and then Fayerweather may make some brief—underlined *brief*—remarks about my life and works. Do you plan to get up and speak, by the way?

DICK. Me?

HARVEY. You. Do you plan to say anything?

DICK. I hadn't thought, Pop...

HARVEY. Don't, if you don't want to. There's nothing more uncomfortable than a reluctant or unwilling speaker. On the other hand, if you, as my eldest son, were to get on your feet and say a few words of farewell...

DICK. (*Quickly.*) Of course I will, Pop.

HARVEY. Good. Then I'll write you in. (*He writes.*) "Brief remarks by my son Richard." (*Pause; looks up.*) Any idea what you might say?

DICK. No, Pop.

HARVEY. You won't make it sentimental, will you? Brad Hoffmeister's son got up the other day and made some very sentimental remarks about Brad. I didn't like it, and I don't think Brad would have liked it.

DICK. I won't get sentimental, Pop.

HARVEY. Good. (*Pause; shuffles documents; looks up again.*) On the other hand, you won't make any wisecracks, will you?

DICK. Oh, Pop...

HARVEY. You have that tendency, Dick. At Marcie's wedding. And your brother's birthday. You got up and made some very flip remarks about all of us.

DICK. I'm sorry, Pop.

HARVEY. Smart-guy stuff. Too smart, in my opinion. If you plan to get into that sort of thing, perhaps you'd better not say anything at all.

DICK. I won't make any cracks, Pop. I promise.

HARVEY. Thank you. (*Looks at documents; looks up again.*) Because you love us, don't you?

DICK. Yes, Pop.

HARVEY. You love us. You may live a thousand miles away, you may have run off every summer, you may be a terrible letter-writer, but you love us all, just the same. Don't you? You love me.

DICK. (*Touching him.*) Oh yes, Pop! Oh yes! Really! (*Pause.*)

HARVEY. Fine. (*Puts his glasses on again; shuffles through*

66

documents.) Now at the graveside, just the family. I want to be buried beside my brothers and below my mother and father. Leave room for your mother to lie beside me. If she marries again, still leave room. She'll come back at the end.

DICK. All right, Pop.

HARVEY. Invite people back here after the burial. Stay close to your mother. She gets nervous at any kind of gathering, and makes bad decisions. For example, don't let her serve any of the good Beefeater's gin if people simply want to mix it with tonic water. And when they're gone, sit with her. Stay in the house. Don't leave for a few days. Please.

DICK. I promise, Pop. (*Annie, the Maid from the first scene, now quite old, adds candlesticks and a lovely flower centerpiece to the table.*)

HARVEY. (*Putting documents back in the envelope.*) And that's my funeral. I'm leaving you this room, you know. After your mother dies, the table and chairs go to you. It's the best thing I can leave you, by far.

DICK. Thanks, Pop. (*Annie exits into the kitchen.*)

HARVEY. Now we'll rejoin your mother. (*He gets slowly to his feet.*) I'll put this envelope in my safe deposit box, on top of my will and the stock certificates. The key will be in my left bureau drawer. (*He starts out, then stops.*) You didn't see the purple finch feeding its young.

DICK. (*Remaining in his chair.*) Yes I did, Pop.

HARVEY. You saw it while I was talking?

DICK. That's right.

HARVEY. Good. I'm glad you saw it. (*He goes out slowly. Dick waits a moment, lost in thought, and then replaces the chairs. The lights come up on the table, now beautifully set with white linen, crystal goblets, silver candlesticks, flowers, the works. Annie begins to set plates as a Hostess—Ruth—comes in from R.*)

RUTH. (*Surveying the table.*) Oh Annie! It looks absolutely spectacular.

ANNIE. Thank you, Mrs.

RUTH. (*As she begins to distribute place cards carefully around the table.*) Now make sure the soup plates are hot.

ANNIE. I always do, Mrs.

RUTH. But I think we can dispense with butter-balls. Just give everyone a nice square of butter.

ANNIE. I'll do butter-balls, Mrs.

RUTH. Would you? How nice! And keep an eye on the ashtrays, Annie. Some people still smoke between courses, but they don't like to be reminded of it.

ANNIE. I know, Mrs.

RUTH. And let's see.... Oh yes. Before people arrive, I want to pay you. (*She produces two envelopes from the sideboard.*) For you. And for Velma in the kitchen. It includes your taxi. So you can both just leave right after you've cleaned up.

ANNIE. Thank you, Mrs.

RUTH. There's a little extra in yours, Annie. Just a present. Because you've been so helpful to the family over the years.

ANNIE. Thank you, Mrs.

RUTH. And now I'd better check the living room.

ANNIE. Yes, Mrs. (*Ruth starts out R., then stops.*)

RUTH. Oh Annie. I heard some strange news through the grapevine. (*Annie looks at her.*) Mrs. Rellman told me that you won't be available any more.

ANNIE. No, Mrs.

RUTH. Not even for us, Annie. We've used you more than anyone.

ANNIE. I'm retiring, Mrs.

RUTH. But surely special occasions, Annie. I mean, if we're desperate. Can I still reach you at your nephew's?

ANNIE. He's moving away, Mrs.

RUTH. But then where will you go? What will you do?

ANNIE. I've got my sister in Milwaukee, Mrs.

RUTH. But we'll be lost without you, Annie.

ANNIE. You'll manage, Mrs.

RUTH. (*Indicating the table.*) But not like this. We'll never match this.

ANNIE. Thank you, Mrs.

RUTH. I think I heard the bell.

ANNIE. I'll get it, Mrs.

RUTH. Women's coats upstairs, men's in the hall closet.

ANNIE. Yes, Mrs. (*Annie starts out.*)

RUTH. Annie! (*Annie stops. Ruth goes to her and hugs her. Annie responds stiffly.*) Thank you, Annie. For everything.

ANNIE. You're welcome, Mrs. (*Annie goes off R., to answer the door. Ruth goes to the sideboard, gets a book of matches. She lights the two candles on the table as she speaks to the audience.*)

RUTH. Lately I've been having this recurrent dream. We're giving this perfect party. We have our dining room back, and Grandmother's silver, before it was stolen, and Charley's mother's royal blue dinner plates, before the movers dropped them, and even the finger bowls, if I knew where they were. And I've invited all our favorite people. Oh I don't mean just our old friends. I mean everyone we've ever known and liked. We'd have the man who fixes our Toyota, and that intelligent young couple who bought the Payton house, and the receptionist at the doctor's office, and the new teller at the bank. And our children would be invited, too. And they'd all come back from wherever they are. And we'd have two cocktails, and hot hors d'oeuvres, and a first-rate cook in the kitchen, and two maids to serve, and everyone would get along famously! (*The candles are lit by now.*) My husband laughs when I tell him this dream. "Do you realize," he says, "what a party like that would cost? Do you realize what we'd have to *pay* these days for a party like that?" Well, I know. I know all that. But sometimes I think it might almost be worth it. (*The rest of the Cast now spills into the dining room, talking animatedly, having a wonderful time. There is the usual gallantry and jockeying around as people read the place cards and find their seats. The Men pull out the Women's chairs, and people sit down. The Host goes to the sideboard, where Annie has left a bottle of wine in a silver bucket. He wraps a linen napkin around it, and begins to pour people's wine. The conversation flows as well. The lights begin to dim. The Host reaches his own seat at the head of the table, and pours his own wine. Then he raises his glass.)*

HOST. To all of us. (*Everyone raises his or her glass. As their glasses go down, the lights fade to black. The table is bathed in its own candlelight. Then the two D. actors unobtrusively snuff the candles, and the play is over.*)

THE END

SUGGESTED IDEAS FOR SMALL TALK AT THE END OF THE PLAY

First Actress (Hostess:)
1. Come in, come in. Are you famished? I hope so. We've got four courses tonight, and I don't want to hear any talk about diets or calories or cholesterol.
2. I've even put place cards. I've arranged it so husbands and wives can't sit together. With six it's easy. My mother used to spend hours arranging the seating for a dinner of twelve.
3. Do you like the candleabra? Do you think they're too much? I dug them out of the attic. They belonged to my great-grandmother, and I thought tonight we'd really splurge.
4. Now be kind to me on the food. I bought the new Julia Childs cookbook, and decided to go whole hog. Thank God for Annie. I don't think there's anyone else in the city who knows how to serve.

Second Actress:
1. This does it! I give up! From here on in, it's hamburgers in the kitchen for me. Ruth, you should go to Washington. They should set you up at the White House. They should make you Secretary of Dinner Parties.
2. Place cards yet! Now where am I sitting? I didn't bring my glasses. Here? Really? (*To Second actor.*) For some strange reason, I'm sitting next to you.
3. (*To second actor.*) Now I want to hear all about you. I hear you've done very well. Do you think the company will move you? No? You mean you'll be here? Well that's lucky. No, I mean it. I'm really very glad you're going to be here.

71

4. (*To Second Actor.*) Oh Lord, here comes the wine. Now stop me if I drink too much. I feel like going overboard tonight. My children are sleeping over at my mother's, and so I'm on my own. Keep an eye on me, for God's sake, so I don't say and do things I'll be sorry for later.

Third Actress:

1. Oh my what a lovely table. How do you do it, Ruth? I try and try, but it never comes out like this. Someone should take a picture. I should have brought my camera. This should be preserved for posterity.
2. Now where do I sit? Ah, right here. You know I used to sit at this place when I was a little girl. Right next to my Daddy. Oh God, what memories. It's my favorite spot. Ruth you put me at my favorite place.
3. I wish my children could see this table. They have no idea what a good table looks like. We've tried to tell them, but they don't care. They don't know what they're missing.
4. What kind of wine is that? It looks like lovely wine. I'm just beginning to learn about wine. I've bought books on it. It's a whole science. We're thinking of going to France just to taste wines.

First Actor (Host):

1. And here we are! Come in, come in! Ruth, you've outdone yourself. I don't know how she does it. She was out all afternoon doing something for the Art Gallery, and then suddenly she produces this. It just seems to appear. Like magic.
2. Now find your seats, everyone. Ruth has all that figured out very carefully. I stay out of that department. All I know is that I'm sitting next to the two loveliest women in town.
3. Now the wine I do know something about. I won't tell you what it is, but I had quite a discussion with Simmons down at the liquor store. It's a special shipment from the Loire Valley, and Ruth and I got the name of it when we were there last spring. So let's try it, and discuss it, and if

we don't like it, I'll bring out something else.
4. Now is everybody seated? Is everybody happy? Then let me simply raise my glass: "To all of us."

Second Actor:
1. Good God, this is too much. It's like a dream. What was that movie? "The Discreet Charm of the Bourgeoisie." Did you see that? That's where we are. We're in that movie.
2. *(To Second Actress)* I hope I'm sitting next to you. Yep. Here we are. Good old Ruth. Do you think she's trying to match us up?
3. How are things going by the way? Are you getting along since your husband left? Are the kids O.K.? Do you like your job? Any chance we could have lunch some day? We've got a lot to talk about.
4. Ah the wine. You always get good wine in this house. I don't know whether it's French or Californian, but it's the best. Most people don't pay much attention to the wine but here, they do.

Third Actor:
1. Wow, what a spread! What is this? Versailles? This is incredible. Ruth, I haven't seen anything like this for years.
2. I actually flew back from Denver for this party. Grabbed an earlier plane. Wouldn't have missed it. I figured you were putting on the dog, and I wanted to get in on it. My God, I should have worn my tuxedo.
3. Can't wait to see what's on the menu. You're the best cook in town, Ruth. I still remember that soufflée thing we had the last time we were here.
4. I hope you noticed I held off on the hors d'oeuvres. I was trying to save room. Except for those bacon things. You should have kept them away from me. I must have eaten ten. No matter. I'll play three sets of tennis tomorrow, and work them off.

last time I... were her...
4. I hope you... afraid... hold on... the Lois' discover? I...
I'm... save some. But it's... I might... I might...
should have kept them as... I...
no. No matter, I'll play... now... we'll... about...
apart... not on?

Set and Prop Pieces

Dining room table
10 matching chairs
8 x 10 rug—*optional*
Mirror
Sideboard
Sconces

Preset on stage:

2 silver candlesticks on sideboard framing mirror with candles
Centerpiece—center of dining room table
In sideboard:
2 hot pads (Sc. 4)
2 linen placemats (durable yet pretty) (Sc. 4)
1 silver salt spoon (Sc. 2)
2 linen placemats (diff. from above) (Sc. 3)
2 reg. spoons (Sc. 3)
1 bell (Sc. 3)
2 envelopes (Sc. 18)
Book of matches (Sc. 18)

Sc. 1
Folder
Purse

Sc. 2
Salt spoon from sideboard

Sc. 3
Round silver tray with doily
2 cups and saucers

74

O.J. glass on sm. plate (also used for Sc. 5)
Creamer on sm. plate
Silver coffee server
Rectangle wooden tray
Buffalo newspaper—inside section with funnies and women's
   section
      (NOTE: All china used in play should be of the same
      pattern)

Sc. 4
   Briefcase
   Typewriter with clean paper
   Pencil
   Book
   3 x 5 cards
   White out

Sc. 5
   Small notebook
   Pencil

Sc. 6
   8 pieces of silver flatware
   Felt silver holder with individual spaces
   Polish rag

Sc. 7
   Grease pencil—black
   Floor plan (3) with sm. rubber band
   Yellow legal tablet
   Glasses for D.R.
   Tape measure—25 to 50 ft. (quiet one if possible)
   Small notebook and pencil

Sc. 8
   Large rectangle utility tray

Preset on tray:
    4 party plates with 4 party napkins
    4 plastic spoons
    4 sm. party hats
    4 party favors without noises
    Wedding ring
    Cake platter/knife
    Ice cream bowl/spoon

Sc. 9
    2 placemats—semi stiff
    2 reg. forks
    2 luncheon plates

Sc. 10
    Eye glasses for Margery, on neck chain
    Swiss army knife

Sc. 11
    6 dinner plates
    Silver carving knife and fork
    Silver turkey platter

Sc. 12
    2 glasses—tall ones
    Beefeaters gin bottle
    Smirnoff vodka bottle

Sc. 13
    Silver round tray
    2 cups and saucers (same from Sc. 3)
    Creamer (same from Sc. 3)
    Sugar holder
    2 reg. spoons (same from Sc. 3)
    Silver teapot
    Duffel bag

tea to pour

empty container

for milk

JEN

Sc. 14
Camera—35 mm
Light meter
Silver round tray (same from Sc. 3)
Silver spoon with rat-tail back
Silver 3 prong fork
Silver pistol handle knife
Silver pistol handle butter knife
Linen placemat with matching napkin
Staffordshire dinner and butter plate
Steuben wine glass
Waterford water glass
Waterford finger bowl

Sc. 15
3 glasses—short, wide ones
Pocketwatch

Sc. 16
Soup tureen

Sc. 17
Glasses for Harvey in a case
Legal size envelop
Preset in envelope:
    2 obituaries
    1 funeral service
    1 picture 3 x 5 of actor playing Harvey

Sc. 18
Bottle of wine
Crystal or silver wine holder
1 linen cloth for wine
Linen off-white tablecloth
Rectangular tray (same from Sc. 3)

Preset on tray:

6 sets of silver—forks, knives, and spoons

Silver round tray (same from Sc. 3)

Preset on tray:

6 crystal wine glasses

2 silver salt servers with 2 silver salt spoons

2 silver pepper shakers

2 silver ashtrays

2 sm. boxes of matches

2 silver candlesticks

Silver centerpiece with artificial flowers

6 dinner plates

6 linen table napkins

6 place cards

Bring

Make

need / silverware

Costume Plot

1st ACTOR

Maroon V neck sweater
3 pc. navy suit
Blue and gold tie
White shirt
Navy nylon socks
Black shoes
White handkerchief
Black belt
Gray cardigan

2nd ACTOR

Raincoat
Brown tweed jacket
Blue check shirt
Brown wool slacks
Brown socks
Brown belt
Navy tie
Cordovan loafers

3rd ACTOR:

Navy wool jacket
Plum wool slacks
Blue and red tie
Light blue Brooks Brothers shirt
Navy socks
Brown shoes
Black belt

1st ACTRESS:
   Raincoat
   Maroon silk drtss with belt
   Maroon slip
   Gray shoes
   Pearl earrings

2nd ACTRESS:
   Purple blue wool skirt
   Royal blue silk blouse
   Navy pumps
   White apron

3rd ACTRESS:
   Blue check wool dress with tie
   Beige tie shoes

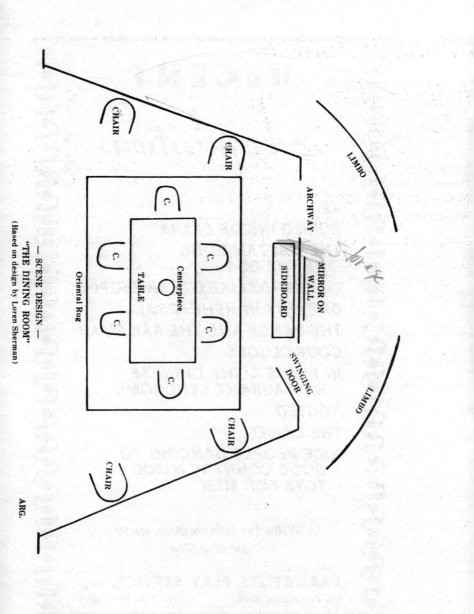

— SCENE DESIGN —
"THE DINING ROOM".
(Based on design by Loren Sherman)

81

RECENT

Acquisitions

K2

BURIED INSIDE EXTRA

**THE TIBETAN BOOK
   OF THE DEAD**

WEEKENDS LIKE OTHER PEOPLE

DREYFUS IN REHEARSAL

THE DANCE AND THE RAILROAD

COUP/CLUCKS

**IN PLACE & THE CHINESE
   RESTAURANT SYNDROME**

ROUTED

THE CAMEO

**NICE PEOPLE DANCING TO
   GOOD COUNTRY MUSIC &
   TOYS FOR MEN**

Write for information as to
availability

DRAMATISTS PLAY SERVICE, Inc.
440 Park Avenue South   New York, N.Y. 10016

New
PLAYS

THE GOLDEN AGE

POPKINS

THAT'S IT FOLKS!

THE RELUCTANT ROGUE

THE RISE AND RISE OF DANIEL ROCKET

RECKLESS

**SECOND PRIZE: *TWO* MONTHS
IN LENINGRAD**

OTHER PLACES

HAUNTED LIVES

GRACELAND & ASLEEP ON THE WIND

FOREVER YOURS MARIE-LOU

DRAMATISTS PLAY SERVICE, INC.
440 PARK AVENUE SOUTH   NEW YORK, N.Y. 10016

NEW Plays

ISN'T IT ROMANTIC

THE HARVESTING

LEVITATION

THE HOUSEKEEPER

BLACK ANGEL

FABLES FOR FRIENDS

SALLY AND MARSHA

THROCKMORTON, TX 76083

DREAMS OF FLIGHT

THE DEATH OF KING PHILIP

SOAP OPERA; WARM AND TENDER LOVE;
GIRLS WE HAVE KNOWN

DRAMATISTS PLAY SERVICE, INC.
440 PARK AVENUE SOUTH   NEW YORK, N.Y. 10016

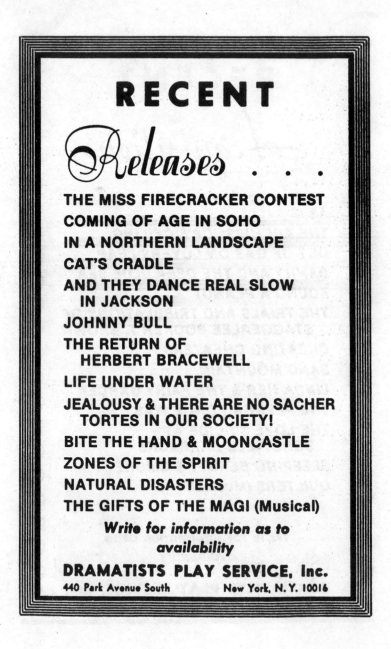